DO NOT HINDER THEM

A Biblical Examination of Childhood Conversion

Justin Peters

Copyright © 2017 Justin Peters Ministries

All rights reserved. No part of this book may be reproduced in any form without written permission from the publisher.

ISBN: 978-1541097698

First Edition

Scripture quotations taken from the New American Standard Bible® (NASB), Copyright © 1960, 1962, 1963, 1968, 1971, 1972, 1973, 1975, 1977, 1995 by The Lockman Foundation
Used by permission. www.Lockman.org

Jim Osman, editor

Cover design: Stephen Melniszyn
Interior layout: John L. Manning

Dedication

This book is dedicated to my wife, Kathy, whom God has used in my life to impact me in ways I could not have imagined before meeting her. She is an iron-sharpener, a source of tremendous encouragement, and is a loving helpmeet. Without her this work may never have come to fruition. By God's grace, in Kathy I truly have found a good thing and obtained favor from the Lord (Proverbs 18:22).

"Justin Peters has written a challenging and compelling book for Christian parents to read and consider as they share the Gospel with their children. By using the authority of God's Word in the New Testament, Justin identifies some of the unbiblical practices that are producing false converts in the church. His book, *Do Not Hinder Them*, is doctrinally sound and instructive for those who read and apply it. I highly recommend it to parents who desire to evangelize their children God's way and to protect them from those who seek to do it man's way."

Evangelist Mike Gendron
Proclaiming the Gospel Ministry
proclaimingthegospel.org

"In this book Justin Peters uses clear thinking and theological accuracy coupled with his gracious demeanor to tackle a subject that, unfortunately, few Christians have thoroughly contemplated. The American Church with its modern approach to gospel proclamation is producing an alarming number of false converts. Sadly, we are doing this to our own children! This must stop! Justin has done a superb job of calling attention to the weak theology, careless thinking, and unbiblical methodology that is inoculating our children against true salvation."

Jim Osman
Pastor/Teacher
Kootenai Community Church
Kootenaichurch.org

"I have been a pastor for 33 years and have seen many times the exact scenario that Justin warns about in this excellent book. It is understandable for parents and church leaders to want to believe that the little ones in their midst are saved when they make a profession of faith but such situations require immense wisdom. This book is a very helpful resource to assist in that wisdom. I wholeheartedly recommend this insightful work by Justin Peters."

Dr. Bryan Hughes
Pastor, Grace Bible Church
Bozeman, Montana
gbcmt.org

"*Do Not Hinder Them*, is a well thought out book that highlights characteristics of a child from the human and spiritual standpoint that legitimately raises the question if a child can truly understand the Gospel. From a scriptural perspective, as Justin points out, children lack a genuine grasp of doctrinal issues relative to salvation. Justin's many years of studying error in the church today has been a blessing to many and this book will be a good addition to bring correction to the contemporary church on this issue. We highly recommend, *Do Not Hinder Them*."

Doug Heck
Pastor, Grace Community Church
Broken Arrow, Oklahoma
gccoftulsa.blog

Susan Heck
withthemaster.com

Table of Contents

Foreword..9

Introduction...15

1. Laying the Groundwork..19

2. The Nature of Children and Salvation: A Study in Contrasts............35

3. Heading Our Homes...57

4. Looking for Fruit: How to Know When Salvation has Come............67

5. Guidance from the Biblical Record...................................85

Conclusion...109

About the Author..113

Foreword

It is of course the solemn duty of all believing parents to instruct their children about both the commandments and the promises of God. Scripture suggests we are to teach them in the same way the apostle Paul said he taught the Ephesians (Acts 20:27, 31)—lovingly but unceasingly admonishing them day and night (with tears when necessary), never shrinking from the task of declaring the whole counsel of God to them.

When God gave the law to Old Testament Israel, His call to faith (the Sh'ma Yisrael) began with a declaration of who He is, followed by the first and great commandment: "The LORD is our God, the LORD is one! You shall love the LORD your God with all your heart and with all your soul and with all your might" (Deuteronomy 6:4-5). The next two sentences are a formal charge to parents: "These words, which I am commanding you today, shall be on your heart. You shall teach them diligently to your sons and shall talk of them when you sit in your house and when you walk by the way and when you lie down and when you rise up" (vv. 6-7).

Notice the stress on careful instruction, continuity, repetition, and hands-on, sustained tutelage. The New Testament command to fathers has similar implications: "Bring them up in the discipline and instruction of the Lord" (Ephesians 6:4). "Discipline" and "instruction" are prolonged undertakings requiring long-term consistency—not in a heavy-handed way that provokes them to wrath, but with heartfelt lovingkindness and joy. Parents seeking to "train up a child in the way he should go" (Proverbs 22:6) cannot outsource the task—nor should they think their evangelistic duty is complete the first time their toddler shows an interest in heaven or says "I love Jesus."

It is an unhappy fact that childhood conversions often fail to produce any genuine spiritual fruit. It is all too easy to talk little children into a false or superficial profession of faith. When that happens, the child will abandon the faith in later years. And it seems to be happening nowadays on an unprecedented scale.

The problem stems first of all from a massive erosion of evangelical conviction among those who self-identify as evangelicals. I've written a number of books pointing out how pervasive (and how corrosive) this problem is. The true gospel of Jesus Christ has all but disappeared in some of largest, most rapidly growing quarters of the evangelical movement. In its place two extremely superficial, emotionally-driven, man-centered brands of religion have begun to dominate. One is the prosperity gospel. The chief prophets of this idea are clearly more concerned about money and material prosperity in this life than they are about Christ and eternity. Another popular variation on the same theme is the seeker-sensitive movement, where the unvarnished biblical gospel has been subjugated to a marketing strategy. Although some of the leading voices in the seeker-sensitive movement occasionally give verbal assent to the authority of Scripture, they clearly are convinced that pragmatism, psychology, public relations, and political correctness are the real keys to winning the world for Christ. If they speak of the gospel at all, it is a truncated message about how Jesus offers purpose and fulfillment in life. It is identical in that regard to the prosperity gospel. (Indeed, the two movements have lately begun to blend together.)

Neither of those alternative "gospels" has much if anything to say about sin, repentance, the sinner's guilt, the cost of atonement, or the lordship of Christ—all essential gospel truths. Instead, the artificial gospels promise eternal life without calling anyone to turn from sin, and they offer assurance of salvation to people who have never felt the weight of personal guilt or sensed any need for forgiveness. They speak of grace merely as a get-out-of-hell free ticket. They have therefore filled churches with false converts—people who think they are Christians but have no true knowledge of Christ as Lord and Savior.

That trend reflects what has been happening in evangelical children's work for decades. Since at least the early twentieth century, child psychology (rather than Scripture itself) has governed how and what evangelicals teach their children. Most of the standard methods of evangelizing children employ a version of the gospel that has been deliberately abridged in order to remove every mention of anything unpleasant or hard to hear. Topics like human depravity, death, divine judgment, personal culpability, and Jesus' warnings about hell are carefully airbrushed out of the message or heavily disguised with sweet-sounding terminology. Guilt (if mentioned at all) is said to be a bad thing because it makes the child feel bad. Sin is spoken of as a mistake or a poor decision. The child is led to believe that God is not angry with our wrong choices; He is merely disappointed and sad. The gist of this toned-down message is that everything wrong can be fixed if we just pray and invite Jesus into our hearts.

That's truly as deep as the average evangelical Sunday school class or Vacation Bible School will go with children these days. Young kids are coached by well-meaning adults, who lead them in reciting a formula prayer. Children who do as they have been prompted are then told they should never question whether they are truly saved. Most have no clue what it means to trust Christ as Savior. Christ is no more real to them than an imaginary friend. But they are encouraged by adults to consider themselves born again because they raised a hand or recited the prayer they were given. It is all too easy to coax "decisions" like that from compliant children. And those who measure ministry success by numbers depend heavily on children's ministry to add professions of faith to the annual count. So the quick-and-dirty approach is regarded by many as a huge success.

There are also voices within the evangelical movement who teach that saving faith is only that initial moment of assent, no matter how ephemeral. Their doctrine is a twisted species of antinomianism, suggesting that faith and obedience are unrelated. Faith, by their reckoning, is an intellectual choice—a "decision" to invite Jesus in or to make a profession of faith. And when someone "accepts Jesus" in childhood but abandons the faith as a teenager, they insist it proves nothing about whether that person was ever truly saved or not.

That is contrary to 1 John 2:19, where John, writing about such traitors to Christ, says, "They went out from us, but they were not really of us; for if they had been of us, they would have remained with us; but they went out, so that it would be shown that they all are not of us." In other words, those who fall away from the faith are in the same category as Judas; they never truly believed in the first place.

For all those reasons, gospel ministry to children must be done with special care, thoroughness, and patient persistence—precisely what the biblical mandates to parents call for.

Are we suggesting that children cannot be saved? Are all childhood conversions invalid? Do we believe parents should not bother encouraging their children to make professions of faith? Of course that is not the point. Children should be urged to trust Christ, and when they are given a proper understanding of the gospel, many do respond to the gospel message with real, permanent, life-transforming faith. In fact, true saving faith is simple, childlike trust in Christ from the heart of those who sense their helplessness, confess their guilt, and perceive their need for a Savior. Jesus Himself said that childlikeness is an essential quality of all real faith. To the adults, He said, "Unless you turn and become like children, you will never enter the kingdom of heaven" (Matthew 18:3).

Samuel, David, and John the Baptist are all examples of believers who came to faith as children. I first trusted Christ as a young child, and my faith has never wavered. My conviction has deepened. My awareness of my need for grace is more acute. My understanding has grown. I don't wrestle with assurance the way I sometimes did as a child. All those things are proper fruits of authentic faith. They are the natural and inevitable result when true childlike faith comes to maturity.

But it is a very serious mistake for parents to imagine that every childhood profession of faith is a bona fide expression of saving trust in Christ. The fruit of faith—not merely a profession of faith—is what parents should look for as evidence that the child's heart is truly regenerate.

Justin Peters understands these issues far better than most. Having made a profession of faith and been baptized at age seven, he never turned against the faith or publicly brought dishonor on the gospel. In fact, he attended seminary, earned two degrees, and entered full-time ministry. But he had little or no understanding about his own need for repentance, and he never enjoyed true settled assurance. That all changed in 2011 when he stepped away from ministry for a time and seriously faced his uncertainties in light of what Scripture teaches about real faith, humble repentance, and the Holy Spirit's work in drawing people to Christ and giving them a new heart.

Having come to Christ with true faith and thereby gained the assurance he once lacked, Justin is uniquely qualified to write on these issues. I'm very grateful for this book, which I know will be a great help to parents, a welcome encouragement to everyone who ministers to young people, and a wonderful resource for adults and young people alike who want to make certain their faith is real and their grasp of gospel truth is accurate.

Dr. John MacArthur
Pastor-Teacher, Grace Community Church
Sun Valley, California

Introduction

Being a pastor—a good pastor—is one of the most difficult jobs (to use that term) in the world. Though there are certainly challenges that I face as an itinerant preacher and Bible teacher, I do not face the kinds of challenges that a pastor faces. If all a pastor had to do was to prepare and preach one doctrinally sound, expositional[1] sermon per week, that, in and of itself, would be a full time job. Most people do not realize how much work expositional preaching demands. It is by far the pastor's most important and solemn task. Pastors, of course, are called upon to do far more than just preach. Pastors, especially those of smaller churches, are expected to visit the sick, attend various meetings, perform weddings and funerals, and at times even be the church janitor. The expectations placed upon them is almost endless.

One day several years ago I asked a friend of mine who pastors a church in Texas, "What is the most challenging thing you face as a pastor?" With barely a second's hesitation he replied, "Knowing when to baptize children." This was not at all the answer I was expecting. He went on to explain that it is very difficult to discern if a child has simply understood some basic elements of the Gospel and professes to believe them or if genuine conversion has taken place. My friend said that he has baptized many children in his ministry who truly seemed to

---

[1] Expositional preaching is that which focuses upon explaining (expositing) the meaning of the text of Scripture. It is typically done verse by verse which, if done properly, necessitates that both the direction and content of the sermon is determined by the text itself. This serves to both minimize the preacher's intentional or unintentional theological biases and maximize the impact of the text on the hearers.

understand the Gospel only to have these same children, years later as teenagers or young adults, walk away from their childhood faith, showing little to no evidence of truly having been made regenerate in Christ. This concerned him greatly, and yet he had no clear solution.

That conversation was, I suppose, the genesis of my interest in this subject. In the years since, I have spoken with numerous pastors from all over the United States who also face this very same dilemma. In fact, my ministry has taken me all over the world and pastors in Australia, Europe, Africa, Asia, and Central and South America tell me much the same thing. These pastors give me the same stories; the only significant difference being their location. I have discovered that this is far from just an American quandary.

In addition to pastors, I have also spoken with numerous Christian parents who are either currently wrestling with this issue or believe they made a mistake and allowed their children to be baptized too early. Many of these parents have told me of their struggles through tears. They love their children deeply and want more than anything to do what is best for them and right before the Lord, but they are unsure of the right thing to do regarding their baptism. It is hard to blame them for their uncertainty.

Ever since the revivalist Charles Finney[2] popularized decisional regeneration and altar calls, evangelicalism has been producing large numbers of baptisms, but far fewer truly transformed lives. Nowhere is the discrepancy between baptisms and transformed lives more pronounced

---

[2]Charles Finney (1792-1875) is widely regarded as the father of modern revivalism and embodied the clear shift from Calvinism to Arminianism in evangelical theology. He referred to the imputation of Christ's righteousness as "theological fiction" [Finney, Charles. *The Memoirs of Charles Finney: The Complete Restored Text* (Grand Rapids, MI: Academie, 1989), pg. 58] and embraced the heresy of Pelagianism which denies original sin and holds that man can willfully choose God apart from any Divine aid. As a revivalist, he was known for eliciting large numbers of "decisions," but, by his own admission, little if any evidence of true conversions. The New England region in which Finney conducted most of his revivals became known as the "burnt-over districts" because of the spiritual coldness left in Finney's wake; a spiritual coldness that remains to this day.

than when dealing with children. Though the statistics are hard to quantify,[3] a startlingly high percentage of children who are raised in evangelical, Bible affirming churches and who make professions of personal faith in Jesus Christ at early ages show little to no evidence of genuine conversion once they leave home and enter their young adult lives.

At this point, let me go ahead and lay my cards on the table. You may have already begun to notice that the direction this book seems to be going is a bit incongruous with the title, *Do Not Hinder Them*. With a title like that, dealing with a subject like this, one might expect this book to argue in favor of teaching children the Gospel and baptizing them at an early age. On the first of these endeavors, it most certainly will. On the latter, it will not.

This work is intended to lay out a biblical and theological case that though we are to raise our children in the "discipline and instruction of the Lord" (Ephesians 6:14), we should wait to baptize them until they are no longer children. The nature of children, the nature of genuine conversion, the biblical and historical record, and simple observation all argue strongly that baptism should be reserved for those who have demonstrated an adult level of both comprehension and appropriation of the Gospel.

---

[3]Ken Ham, author of *Already Gone* (Master Books: Green Forest, AR), presents sobering research documenting the high percentage of children who, after having been raised in evangelical churches, leave church once they leave home.

1
Laying the Groundwork

To say that this book will go against the evangelical grain would be quite the understatement. The premise presented in the following pages is completely foreign to probably upwards of 95% of evangelical churches. Given that there is such an imposing mountain of misunderstanding that must be conquered, let us begin by laying some groundwork.

Billy's Problem

Billy has a problem. Here's the scenario: Little "Billy" is raised in a Christian home, attends Sunday School, hears in both settings the basics of the Gospel and begins to ask questions about salvation and how to become a Christian. Because his parents have been praying for his salvation since he was born, they are both eager to help him and thankful they have this opportunity. They tell him that he needs to admit that he is a sinner, believe that Jesus died on the cross and then rose from the dead, and ask Jesus to forgive him of his sins and be his personal Lord and Savior. Billy says that he wants to do this.

Aware that Billy is young and wanting to make sure that his decision is real, Billy's parents call the church office to schedule an appointment with their pastor. The pastor is quite happy to help this family and speak with young Billy.

On the appointed day, the pastor welcomes Billy and his parents into his office and talks with them. The boy's parents tell the pastor that Billy has been asking questions about how to become a Christian and expressing a desire to be baptized. After listening to his parents, the pastor turns his attention to Billy and asks Billy to tell him in his own words what being a Christian means.

Billy explains that he knows that he is a sinner and has done things that displease God. He says that he believes that Jesus is the Son of God and died on the cross to pay the penalty for sin. He believes Jesus was raised from the dead on the third day, and there is no salvation apart from trusting in Him and repenting of sin.

The pastor is careful not to put any words in Billy's mouth. Both he and his parents want to make sure that Billy knows what he is doing, so they let the child speak on his own. Though he speaks as any child would, he does seem to grasp the basics of the Gospel and expresses a sincere desire to become a Christian.

Therefore, the pastor, with the grateful consent of the parents says, "Ok, Billy, let's pray, and I just want you to talk to Jesus in your own words and ask Him to save you." Billy does just that and is quite sincere.

At the end of the service the next Sunday morning, Billy and his parents walk down the aisle at the time of invitation and stand beside the pastor. The pastor shares with the congregation how he and the parents have spent time with Billy answering his questions and making sure Billy understands his decision to follow Christ. The pastor asks the congregation, "If you join me in welcoming Billy into the family of God and as a member of our church, please signify your approval by saying 'Amen.'" The congregation responds with a collective, "Amen." The pastor says, "I'm sure there are none opposed." There are, of course, none.

Either the next Sunday or one very soon thereafter, Billy stands in the baptistery with the pastor. With parents and other immediate and extended family members watching in the pews, the pastor asks,

"Billy, do you recognize that you are a sinner and believe that Jesus died on the cross to save you from your sins?"

"Yes."

"Have you received Jesus Christ as your personal Lord and Savior?"

"Yes."

"Upon your profession of faith, Billy, I baptize you, my brother, in the name of the Father, and of the Son, and of the Holy Spirit." As the pastor lowers Billy's head into the water, he says, "Buried with Him in baptism," and then immediately lifting Billy back out of the water proclaims, "And raised to newness of life!"

The congregation enthusiastically applauds and welcomes Billy into the family of God and as a full member of their local church. All of this typically happens when Billy is between five and ten years of age.

For the next several years things seem fine. Billy continues to attend church and Sunday School, but as he gets into his teenage years, things begin to change. Slowly, but surely, he becomes more and more influenced by his friends, and the allures of the world begin to tug on Billy's heart. Secretly, he begins to do the things he knows are wrong. He drinks and uses coarse language when hanging out with his friends on the weekends, and is tempted by and likely succumbs to premarital sex. Billy is still a nice young man and outward appearances seem fine to most. He still dutifully goes to church with his parents and is even active in the youth group, but…

The tug of the world on Billy's heart grows stronger and stronger.

Billy graduates from high school, goes off to college, and for the first time in his life has some real independence. Dad and mom are no longer around to make him go to church. He either does not attend church at all or goes to one that is a doctrinally weak, seeker-oriented church.[4] The world

---

[4]Seeker oriented or "Seeker Sensitive" churches are those, broadly speaking, which eschew things deemed archaic like hymns and expository preaching in favor of an approach to church that is catered toward the "felt needs" of the unchurched masses. Rick Warren and Bill Hybels, pastors of Saddleback and Willow Creek churches respectively, have been two of the prominent leaders in this movement. They have conducted surveys asking lost people what they want in a church and then designed their churches to meet these felt needs. Expositional preaching was replaced by topical discussions and the music modernized and the services made more entertaining.

and its temptations tug even more strongly on Billy with his newly found independence and there is little, if any, discernable difference between his lifestyle and that of his nonbelieving peers. He is surrounded by a liberal and pluralistic worldview and begins to question the things he was taught as a child growing up in church. Even if he does not give voice to his doubts, they are there.

Eventually, Billy gets married and starts a family. His wild oat sowing days are behind him and, from the outside, Billy's life appears to be going well. However, his church attendance is either non-existent or sporadic. Furthermore, he has no desire to study Scripture, no godly affections, and no godly sorrow over sin. The more rambunctious sins of his adolescence have merely been replaced with more secretive sins. He may be an outwardly nice guy, but there has been no genuine repentance and none of the spiritual fruit that accompanies true conversion. Sound familiar?

There are also multitudinous "Billys" who *are* active in church—very active. They bring their families to church and their kids attend Sunday School and VBS. But their churches are weak. Their churches preach a diluted Gospel largely devoid of any emphasis on sin, repentance, and personal holiness. These churches tolerate or even wink at egregious sin in their midst. Church discipline[5] is foreign to the congregation. Becoming a Christian is reduced to making a verbal profession of faith in Christ absent from any life transformation. The difference between the lives of these church members and those of the world is merely superficial.

---

[5]Church discipline is the first commandment Jesus gave to His church. It is designed to bring a sinning believer to repentance. The steps of church discipline are laid out quite clearly in Matthew 18:15-20, the third of which is telling the entire church of the individual's sin if he has not repented. If upon this third step the individual remains unrepentant, then he has proven himself to be a false convert and is to be put out of the church. Church discipline is just as much a commandment from Christ as is the Lord's Supper (Communion) and Believer's Baptism and yet very, very few evangelical churches practice it.

The common excuse is that Billy is just "backslidden."[6] Far too often this has become the excuse for the person who professes faith in Christ but lives a life characterized by sin. Billy is not backslidden. Billy is lost. Billy is just another of the millions of false converts created by baptizing a young child who simply made intellectual assent to a few basic Bible facts without ever having truly repented of sin and been made alive in Christ. Modern evangelicalism has produced legions of whitewashed tombs.

Statistics are not even necessary to know this is true. Probably all of us have either been a Billy (or Sally) ourselves, or we have them in our families or amongst our friends. We see all around us people who profess to be believers and yet live lives of habitual, unrepentant sin. The difference between the lives of professing believers and unbelievers seems to be diminishing. That there is little difference between how believers and non-believers live is, in fact, one of the primary criticisms levied against Christianity.

This short book is intended to address what I believe to be an extremely important and yet woefully misunderstood issue in modern evangelicalism: specifically, when is it appropriate to baptize a child who makes a profession of faith in Christ?

This book is going to deal with a very sensitive issue for many families. In many ways, with this book I am walking straight into a perfect storm.

Firstly, though there are ample resources out there in dealing with evangelizing children, the vast majority of them, while possibly passing a bare minimal evangelical bar, are just that: minimalistic. They reduce very serious issues such as sin, God's wrath, repentance, grace, faith, and justification to a few simple ABCs. On the LifeWay Christian Bookstores website is an article entitled "Becoming a Christian can be as easy as A-B-C!" in which a person can follow three "easy" steps to become

---

[6]"Backslidden" is not a term used for New Testament believers but rather is used only in reference to Old Testament Israel·

a Christian.[7] This particular article is not even specifically directed toward children but for anyone of any age. The watering down of the Gospel knows no age boundary but it is especially acute in dealing with children.

For example, there is a popular book written to aid parents in evangelizing their children entitled *Lola Mazola's Happyland Adventure: My John 3:16 Book* in which "Happyland" represents Heaven. The description of the book states:

> The adorable title character learns the meaning and truth of John 3:16 in relation to her desperate desire to visit the Happyland theme park. Who wouldn't want to go? Happyland boasts sixty rides, twenty shows, three hotels, two lakes, a water park, and a zoo! After the story, a suggested prayer guides children to receive Christ's promise of salvation and everlasting life, while Lola invites them to sign and date a commemorative certificate, cementing this special moment in their memories.

This is emblematic of one of the most concerning deficiencies regarding this genre of resources. Heaven is presented as a fairytale place full of fun and excitement, the entrance to which is secured simply by reciting a prayer. There is no mention of denial of self, repentance, or counting the costs of following Christ. And, should later in life the child have doubts about his membership to "Happyland," he need not examine himself to make sure that he is in the faith as 2 Corinthians 13:5 instructs. To the contrary, he need only recall filling out that commemorative certificate when he was between four and eight years of age.[8]

---

[7] Source: http://www.lifeway.com/Article/Becoming-a-Christian-can-be-as-easy-as-A-B-C Accessed February 11, 2016. Though the article does have the basic elements of the Gospel, it so minimizes the Gospel's high demands as to be misleading. Further, the article ends by stating, "If I ever wonder if I am a Christian, I can remember this special day when Jesus came into my life to stay!" This is an exceedingly dangerous thing to teach. Scripture instructs, "Test yourselves to see if you are in the faith" (2 Corinthians 13:5). The mark of a believer is obedience to the commands of Christ, not praying a one-time "Sinner's Prayer" (which is not even found in Scripture) and writing down the date it was prayed.

[8] This is the age range author Robert J. Morgan recommends for his book.

Secondly, this book will go against the prevailing practice in the vast, vast majority of evangelical churches. The Gospel has been so watered down for so long that it has not even occurred to most that something beyond intellectual assent to a few basic Gospel facts should be demonstrated by the baptismal candidate. The typical baptismal candidate is simply asked to respond affirmatively to a few basic questions and is then lowered into the waters.

A friend of mine once told me of going to see his seven year old niece baptized at a large Southern Baptist church in Mississippi. This particular service was being held at a local YMCA swimming pool. When the girl waded into the water and stood in front of the church youth minister who was performing the service, he asked her, "Do you promise to make Jesus your forever friend?" The little girl replied, "Yes," and she was baptized to the applause of everyone there; everyone, that is, except my friend.

What a tragedy this was. Not only was it a tremendous disservice to the little girl to make her believe that she is saved because she promised to make Jesus her "forever friend," but it was also blasphemous in its degradation of the Gospel. Though this example is a bit extreme (one would hope) it is nonetheless indicative of a demonstrable lowering of the baptismal bar. Almost all evangelical churches merely ask the baptismal candidates to affirmatively answer a few basic questions before being lowered into and then raised from the water as a public profession of their faith and new life in Christ. This is true for baptismal candidates of any age, adults and children alike. The premise of this book will definitely go against the prevailing evangelical thinking and practice on this issue.

Thirdly, the issue with which this book deals is an extremely sensitive one. All good parents want what is best for their children. There is nothing more precious to them than the physical and spiritual well-being of their little ones. Christian parents make sure their children attend church and participate in Sunday School. They may send them to a private Christian school or even home school them so they can be educated from a biblical worldview and at least somewhat shielded from the corrosive influences of the culture.

When their child begins to express an interest in becoming a Christian, they are encouraged and grateful, yet cautious. Most parents know not to put words into the child's mouth. They know he needs to demonstrate at least some level of understanding of what he is doing. The child certainly *seems* to understand. He answers all of the questions asked of him correctly, even those asked by the pastor. They schedule his baptism and friends and family members all gather for the special day. They genuinely believe they have done everything right and their little boy is now a Christian. This is one of the most special days of their lives.

To then come along and suggest that they have made a mistake by baptizing him and should have waited until much later seems to call into question not only their parenting, but also their own biblical and theological understanding. It appears to question the validity of the child's conversion. It may even call into question the validity of their own baptisms if they, too, were baptized as young children. By extension, the position that will be forwarded in this book potentially calls into question the validity of multiplied tens of millions of childhood baptisms that have been performed in evangelical churches for decades.[9]

Please know that I am aware of just how much against the grain of evangelical thought this book goes. It is an unfortunate reality that practices and beliefs can become so engrained in our ecclesiastical culture that they are simply assumed to be right and true. It must be okay because "we have always done it this way." We often criticize Roman Catholicism[10] for elevating church tradition to the same authoritative

---

[9] Please note that I am not saying that it would necessarily call into question the validity of the *conversions* of all of these individuals but merely their baptisms. I believe that it is undoubtedly the case that millions of people were baptized as children but then later in life, either as teenagers or adults, came to a true saving knowledge of Jesus Christ.

[10] For excellent resources on understanding the heresies of the Roman Catholic Church, please see the ministry of Mike Gendron at: www.proclaimingthegospel.org

level as Scripture, and rightly so. Yet, we as evangelicals have done much the same thing. We, too, have elevated various church traditions to an almost biblical level of authority; not because they are indeed biblical, but because they have become an almost universally accepted part of our church culture. They have been practiced by so many churches for so many years that they practically carry biblical authority. Precious few people would even think there is a need to question them. The few evangelicals who may have doubts about these practices rarely if ever voice them. After all, how could so many be so wrong for so long?

I would contend, though, that the baptism of young children has become one of those traditions. It is has been an evangelical mainstay for well over half a century and there are few alive today who have known anything different. It is as accepted a part of church doctrine and practice as is the Lord's Supper and international missions. To even express a doubt about the practice of baptizing children would sound as foreign to most evangelical ears as it would to express a doubt about the authority of the Scriptures.

And yet, it is precisely a desire to return to the authority of Scripture for all of our beliefs and practices that compels me to write this work. All of us as theologically conservative evangelical Christians appeal to the Bible as the only and final authority for our doctrine and theology and we strive to be as biblical as possible in our orthopraxy.[11] It is time for us to return to the authority of Scripture in this area as well. The baptism of young children is, in my estimation, one of evangelicalism's most tragic departures from sound doctrine.

A Brief Word on Baptism

Baptism has been a bone of contention in the church almost since its inception. The young and immature believers in the church of Corinth were boasting about whom had been baptized by which

---

[11]Orthopraxy refers to correct practice within the church whereas orthodoxy refers to correct doctrine.

Apostle. Even the early church had their issues with "evangelical celebrity"[12] worship. Such a man-centered perspective resulted in divisions in the local body (1 Corinthians 1:12-17). Paul rebuked their childish sectarianism by saying "Christ did not send me to baptize but to preach the Gospel" (vs. 17). This statement is one of many in Scripture that indicates there is a distinction between conversion and the act of baptism.

It is my hope and prayer that this book will be helpful to believers from different theological backgrounds, so let me briefly explain my views on this ordinance. I hold to *credobaptism*. Credobaptism is the theological term given to "believer's baptism;" that baptism is reserved for those who have repented from sin and placed their trust in the risen Lord Jesus Christ and His atoning work on the cross for salvation. Baptism is for people who have been made regenerate by the working of God's Holy Spirit and baptized into the body of Christ.[13] Once this new birth has taken place, believers are to be baptized[14] as an act of obedience to the command of Christ.[15]

An adherence to credobaptism necessitates a rejection of *paedobaptism*, which is the term given to the practice of baptizing infants. The Roman Catholic Church and also some mainline Protestant denominations hold to this practice. Neither the Church of Rome, nor the liberal mainline denominations hold to the basic tenets of the Gospel, so these are to be considered outside of biblical Christianity regardless.

---

[12] The secular world has its celebrities but, unfortunately, so does the evangelical world. Evangelicals will pick some of their favorite preachers and hold them up as spiritual supermen of sorts. Though biblically qualified elders are to be respected (1 Timothy 5:17) the only One Whom should be held above men is Jesus Christ. To quote missionary and preacher Paul Washer, "There is no such thing as a great man of God, only weak, pitiful, faithless men of a great and merciful God." For more information about Paul Washer's ministry see www.heartcrymissionary.com

[13] 1 Corinthians 12:31 states, "For by one Spirit we were all baptized into one body...." This is a reference to the Holy Spirit's work of regenerating and then placing a person into the universal body of Christ.

[14] It is also this author's position that the proper mode of baptism is by immersion in water.

[15] See Matthew 28:16-20 and Acts 2:38-42.

This having been said, there is one denomination, the Presbyterian Church in America (PCA)[16] that certainly *does* fall within biblical Christianity, and yet it practices paedobaptism. The PCA denomination has a high view of Scripture and the sovereignty of God in salvation. Its pastors are committed to expositional preaching. There is no question that they are compatriots in the Gospel and their contribution to evangelical theology has been significant. They do, however, baptize infants. According to the PCA, the visible church is comprised of "all who make profession of their faith in the Lord Jesus Christ, together with their children."[17] The PCA holds that baptized infants need not be re-baptized later in life.[18]

Though I hold many of my PCA brothers in Christ in high esteem and am profoundly grateful for their defense of the Gospel, I do enthusiastically differ with them on this. It is not a matter of salvation or a cause to break fellowship, but I do believe it to be an important issue.

I offer the above very brief descriptions of the various prominent positions on infant baptism just as a point of distinction between what many groups practice and the perspective from which this book is written. When I speak of baptism, I am assuming a belief in credo, or believer's baptism, which is an act of obedience subsequent to the new birth wrought by the Holy Spirit in the life of a sinner.

---

[16] This is not to be confused with the liberal Presbyterian Church USA. The Presbyterian PCA separated from the Presbyterian USA because of the latter's liberal theology including its denial of the deity of Christ and rejection of the inerrancy and authority of Scripture.

[17] PCA Digest, Position Papers, 1973-1998. Source: http://pcahistory.org/pca/2-078.html Accessed February 24, 2016.

[18] The Twelfth PCA General Assembly (1985) Section 13-23, pg. 85: Ad-Interim Committee on Baptism states, "The one presented for Christian baptism as an infant by parents who profess the Christian faith, which parents are later judged to lack a credible profession, has nevertheless received Christian baptism and ought not to be re-baptized." Further, the PCA Westminster Confession of Faith and Catechisms on page 37 states, "The sacrament of baptism is but once to be administered unto any person." Source: http://www.pcaac.org/wp-content/uploads/2012/11/WCFScriptureProofs.pdf

A final word on baptism: some parents with whom I have spoken have expressed concern that if they were to delay their child's baptism and, heaven forbid, something were to happen to him, his eternal destiny would be in doubt. If you have any such fears, please, put them aside. Baptism does not save[19] nor does the lack of it condemn. Those whom God saves He keeps.

Summary

This book is not going to make the argument that God cannot save a child. That is not at all the question. God can and does save whomever He wishes. Neither will this work argue that God, on occasion, does not save a child. I have heard credible testimonies from people who believe they came to a saving knowledge of Christ as a child and since have walked in obedience to Him and borne genuine fruit.

That having been said, this book will make the argument that God is not saving children nearly as often as our baptismal records indicate. We will see that the nature of salvation calls for great care to be taken before baptizing a person of any age. We will see that the nature of children calls for particular care and caution before baptism. We will also see that the history of the early church gives no indication that children were ever baptized, much less that it was the common practice it is today.

This is not at all intended to be a negative book. It is not my intention to throw cold water on anyone's baptism or to criticize anyone's sincerity or parenting skills. As I travel and preach in churches across the United States and abroad, I often make the point that the most loving thing we can do for people in error is to tell them the truth. The most unloving thing we can possibly do is to leave them in error.

Baptizing young children is one of the most serious and yet widely accepted and practiced errors in evangelicalism. It is not an error that is practiced with any intentional malice. Rather, it is an error that is prac-

---

[19]The erroneous belief that baptism is necessary for salvation or makes it effectual is known as "baptismal regeneration." It is actually a very dangerous doctrine for, taken to its logical conclusion, it leads to a works salvation.

ticed subtly because "we've always done it this way," and most have just unquestionably accepted it. Though done without malice, the almost universal acceptance of this practice is, I believe, indicative of a pervasive lack of theological depth among our churches. Topical preaching has usurped exposition's rightful place in the pulpit. An emphasis on the sovereignty of God in salvation has fallen out of favor in light of the impressive numbers that decisional regeneration and Hyper-grace[20] seem to deliver.

The sad reality is that most professing believers are largely biblically illiterate. Sure, many of them are familiar with various biblical stories and can recite some of the basics of the Gospel, but these same individuals have little or no understanding of how to think biblically. They do not have an understanding of biblical hermeneutics[21] or how to apply biblical theology to their lives. They all profess to believe that the Bible is God's Word, but cannot truly evaluate matters from a proper theological perspective.

This inability on the part of most to integrate sound doctrine into either their personal lives or into the life of the church is the product of weak and anemic preaching from most pulpits. Most, though not all,[22] pastors have surrendered to the influences of the culture and succumbed

---

[20]Hyper-grace is the term used to denote the teaching that over emphasizes the grace of God to the exclusion of teaching on sin and repentance. It holds that Christians need not confess their sins before God and are no longer bound by God's moral Law. Hyper-grace teachers such as Joseph Prince hold that 1 John 1:9 which says, "If we confess our sins, He is faithful and righteous to forgive us our sins and cleanse us from all unrighteousness" was not addressed to believers when, in fact, it was. The hyper-grace teaching gives room for professing believers to live in habitual, unrepentant sin; room not afforded by a correct understanding of Scripture.

[21]Hermeneutics is the art and science of Bible interpretation. If one's hermeneutical grid is wrong, then the conclusions to which we come will also be wrong resulting in a wrong understanding of God. Conversely, proper and sound hermeneutics results in the rich reward of rightly understanding God. For a good primer book on hermeneutics, see *How to Study the Bible* by Dr. Richard Mayhue (Christian Focus publishers, 2006).

[22]Though it can get discouraging to see the compromised state of the broad spectrum of visible Christianity, there are good men out there all over the world who are doing the work of a shepherd. Most of these men pastor small churches and are never asked to speak at conferences or conventions. They labor in the Word and shepherd their flocks in anonymity; known only to their congregants—and to God. It has been a great blessing for my wife, Kathy, and me to fellowship with many of these men and their churches in my itinerant preaching ministry.

to the desires of their congregants, many of whom are themselves unconverted. They are not "holding fast the faithful word," and therefore neither they nor their church members can "exhort in sound doctrine and refute those who contradict" (Titus 1:9). Such a state makes it impossible to see issues clearly through the lens of Scripture.

This book is written for pastors. Many are the pastors who have lovingly and wisely counseled parents to wait on baptizing their children only to have these parents respond in anger and frustration. I desire to come alongside our faithful shepherds and metaphorically 'hold up their arms'[23] as they deal with a very difficult and extraordinarily sensitive issue.

This book is written for parents. It is written for all of those believing parents who strive to rear their children biblically. They want to do what is right for their children and what is honoring before the Lord. It is my hope and prayer that this resource will help bring biblical clarity to an issue that is often confusing for them. The subject of when and if to baptize a child has been the victim of poor teaching and held hostage by unquestioned church tradition. It need not be confusing, though. As we shall see, the Word of God is not at all silent on this issue. So, it is my desire to hold the arms of our godly parents up as well.

Much of what follows you may find to be very different from the paradigm with which you were raised and are familiar. It may seem quite foreign and you may find yourself wondering, 'If this book is true, how is it that so many churches have been so wrong for so long?' The truth is that the baptism of young children is done much more from tradition rather than biblical precedent. There is nothing wrong in and of itself with tradition, of course. Tradition should not be discarded simply because it is just that—tradition.

---

[23] This is a reference to Exodus 17 in which Israel, led by Joshua, was fighting the Amalekites. Moses, accompanied by Aaron and Hur, were watching the battle from a nearby hilltop. When Moses held his arms up toward the sky, the Israelites prevailed. When he grew weary and lowered his arms, the Amalekites prevailed. So Aaron and Hur each got under one of Moses' arms and held them up for him until sunset and the Israelites won a great victory.

However, we must take care that our ecclesiastical traditions not run contrary to sound doctrine and theology (Mark 7:13).[24] If there is any area of church life where this has become the case, then we simply must bend our knees to the Scriptures. I invite you to join me now as we look at what the Bible has to say about this important issue.

---

[24] The Pharisees and scribes had a tradition of allowing a son who had become angry with his parents to declare all of his possessions "Corban." As such, the possessions could only be used for sacred purposes and could not be used as financial assistance for his parents. Jesus condemned this tradition because it effectively negated the commandment to honor one's father and mother (Exodus 20:12; Ephesians 6:2).

2

The Nature of Children and Salvation: A Study in Contrasts

The question of when and if to baptize a child represents the confluence of several different issues: the eternal destination of babies and children who die, the nature of children, and the nature of salvation. In this chapter I will seek to provide a brief, but by no means exhaustive, discussion of each.

Babies and Children Who Die

There is surely no greater pain for parents than for one of their children to die at a young age. Parents naturally expect to die before their children, but as we all know, this is not always how life plays out. Babies and young children are just as subject to the effects of living in a fallen world as are adults. Death is an appointment that we will all one day keep (Hebrews 9:27) and, for some, it is an appointment that comes shortly after life begins.

In the six thousand years or so of human history, literally billions of babies born and unborn have died. Estimates are that between 30% and 50% of fertilizations end in miscarriages. There can be no doubt either biblically or scientifically[25] that life begins at the moment of conception. Every conception that has ever occurred in human history represents a real person with a real soul.

---

[25]Upon conception, the fertilized egg performs all of life's functions such as transporting materials, metabolizing energy, growth, reproduction, etc. Its gender is set and has its own DNA separate from and unique to that of his or her mother and father. For more information see
http://naapc.org/why-life-begins-at-conception/

Though not possible to do, if we could somehow add up all of the miscarriages, all of the aborted babies, and all of the infants and children who have died in all of human history, we would arrive at a truly staggering number. Given that each of these persons possesses an eternal soul, the question of what happens to these souls is an important one.

It is tempting to base our theology of the eternal destination of little ones upon emotions and human reasoning. All of us have a natural tenderness toward the very young, and our sympathies toward them incline us to believe that they would surely go to Heaven when they die. The temptation to use human sentimentality as the basis for our theology regarding this question (or any other for that matter) must be resisted. Scripture alone must be the solid foundation for our beliefs.

Though there is not a direct verse on what happens to children when they die, the compendium of biblical teaching argues strongly that they go immediately to Heaven. This is not a position based upon mere feelings, but upon sound biblical doctrine.

God's Disposition Toward Children

God's Word has much to say about how He views children.

- *Every Life Decreed by God*

That life begins at conception is an incontrovertible fact and every single life exists by God's decree. Psalm 22:9-10 states, "Yet You are He Who brought me forth from the womb; You made me trust *when* upon my mother's breasts. Upon You I was cast from birth; You have been my God from my mother's womb." Even if the act which led to the conception was done outside of marriage and, therefore, sinful, God is sovereign over that sin, and it is He Who creates life.

God has a purpose for every life that comes into being. God said to the prophet Jeremiah, "Before I formed you in the womb, I knew you" (Jeremiah 1:4-5). John the Baptist's birth and ministry were foretold by the angel Gabriel (Luke 1:5-17). The Apostle Paul, under the inspiration of God's Holy Spirit, testified that he was set apart from his mother's womb (Galatians 1:15). The testimony of Scripture is clear; that for which God creates He has a foreordained plan.

- *Sinners by Birth But Not Culpable*

The Bible teaches that all of us are sinners by birth, by nature, by choice, and by practice. Romans 5:12 states, "Therefore just as through one man sin entered the world, and death through sin, and so death spread to all men, because all sinned." Once Adam and Eve ate of the forbidden fruit,[26] sin and the propensity to sin were passed on to all of the human race. Each and every human that has ever been conceived post Fall,[27] regardless of whether or not he or she lived to adulthood, inherited a sin nature from our original parents.

We've all seen YouTube clips of young children caught in the act of being naughty. They often feature a young child with some food or paint or both (or worse!) smeared all over himself and all over the floor, walls, carpets, pets, etc. The scene is a total disaster and almost certainly calls for some professionals to come in to clean up the mess. Mom or Dad comes up to the child with video camera rolling and asks the child, "Did you make this mess?" The child looks straight into his parent's eyes, shakes his head and in his sweet little voice unhesitatingly replies, "No."

We think these clips to be cute. And they are! We almost cannot help but laugh and even be endeared toward these little mischief-makers. But these adorable clips reveal a truth that is anything but adorable. They reveal that children do not have to be taught to lie. Children do not have to be taught to be selfish. Sin comes quite naturally for them because their nature is just that—sinful. The inherent sinful nature that leads a child to lie to his parents is the very same nature that can eventually lead an Adolf Hitler, a Joseph Stalin, a Vladimir Lenin, or an Osama Bin Laden to become a mass murderer.

---

[26]Though often portrayed as an apple, the Bible actually does not tell us what the forbidden fruit was.

[27]The Fall refers to the act of Eve and Adam's sin that resulted in all of creation being ruined by sin.

Charles Spurgeon once said, "As the salt flavors every drop in the Atlantic, so does sin affect every atom of our nature. It is so sadly there, so abundantly there, that if you cannot detect it, you are deceived."[28] Sin pervades every fiber of our being. Left in our fallen state, our wills are helplessly predisposed to sin.

This bent toward sin does not begin when one commits his first volitionally sinful act; it begins at conception. In Psalm 51:5 David states, "Behold, I was brought forth in iniquity, and in sin my mother conceived me." Though our sin nature is inherited at conception, our culpability for sinful acts does not come until much later.

Consider the words of God to the Jews who had become so atrociously sinful they were sacrificing their own children to pagan Babylonian gods: "You slaughtered My children" (Ezekiel 16:21). Note that God considered these little ones to be *His*. Similarly, in Jeremiah 2:34 and 19:4 God refers to children as "the innocents." God claimed ownership of these innocent babies.

These children were not exceptions to the sinful nature. They were not born as morally neutral as many assert. They inherited a sinful nature from Adam just as all of us have and they possessed the exact same predilection toward sin. A 1926 Minnesota crime commission stated:

> Every baby starts life as a little savage. He is completely selfish and self-centered: he wants what he wants—his bottle, his mother's attention, his playmate's toys, his uncle's watch, or whatever. Deny him these and he seethes with rage and aggressiveness which would be murderous were he not so helpless. He is dirty; he has no morals, no knowledge and no developed skills. This means that all children, not just certain children, but all children, are born delinquent. If permitted to continue in their self-centered world of infancy, given free reign to their impulsive actions to satisfy each want, every child would grow up a criminal, a killer, a thief, and a rapist.[29]

---

[28]Charles Spurgeon sermon entitled "Honest Dealing with God," preached at the Metropolitan Tabernacle on June 20, 1875.
[29]Source: http://www.wnd.com/2008/11/81872/ Accessed 2016.

This is a startling quote to be sure, but it is biblically accurate. The doctrine of Total Depravity holds that, left to his own vices, every person's will is held in helpless bondage to sin. No one has within himself any inherent righteousness. Every part of man—his mind, will, flesh and emotions—is affected by sin. Our hearts are "deceitful above all things and desperately wicked" (Jeremiah 17:9). It is not that every man is as bad as he could be, but that even his seemingly "good" acts are tainted with sin, and if not for the general restraining power of the Holy Spirit, every single person is fully capable of unspeakable horror.

The biblical reality is that your little bundle of joy is no exception. Children's hearts are "desperately wicked" too. However, they have not committed any volitional sinful acts. And this is a big difference.

Those who spend eternity in Hell do so not because of their sinful nature per se, but rather because of the sinful *acts* that result from that nature.

> *Do not be deceived; neither fornicators, nor idolaters, nor adulterers, nor effeminate, nor homosexuals, nor thieves, nor the covetous, nor drunkards, nor revilers, nor swindlers, will inherit the kingdom of God.*—1 Corinthians 6:9b-10

> *Now the deeds of the flesh are evident, which are immorality, impurity, sensuality, idolatry, sorcery, enmities, strife, jealousy, outbursts of anger, disputes, dissensions, factions, envying, drunkenness, carousing, and things like these…that those who practice such things will not inherit the kingdom of God.*—Galatians 5:19-21.

> *Therefore consider the members of your earthly body as dead to immorality, impurity, passion, evil desire, and greed, which amounts to idolatry. For it is because of these things that the wrath of God will come upon the sons of disobedience*—Colossians 3:5-6.

> *God gave them over to a depraved mind, to do those things which are not proper, being filled with all unrighteousness, wickedness, greed, evil; full of envy, murder, strife, deceit, malice; they are gossips, slanderers, haters of God, insolent, arrogant, boastful, inventors of evil, disobedient to parents, undiscerning*—Romans 1:28-31

These are the works of unbelievers.[30] These works are the bad fruit of one who has "suppressed the truth in unrighteousness" per Romans 1:18. Unbelief in the Gospel is not merely an isolated lack of belief that results in some vague neutrality in morals or actions. Unbelief always manifests itself in unrighteous *deeds*.

A young child can certainly do things that are wrong—even sinful. Children are human after all, and therefore, sinful by nature. However, when a young child lies or fails to clean his room, he is not doing so because he is "suppressing the truth in unrighteousness." He is not knowingly and intentionally violating the moral Law of God. He may understand that he is doing something of which Daddy and Mommy disapprove, but he has no understanding that he has sinned against the thrice holy God.[31]

Though the consequences of one's sin can be felt by others, the guilt is borne solely by the sinner himself. Each person is held responsible for his own sin and only his own sin. Deuteronomy 24:16 states, "Fathers shall not be put to death for their sons, nor shall sons be put to death for their fathers; everyone shall be put to death for his own sin." So even though the young inherit a sinful nature, it is only their future acts of willful sin that earn them the wrath of God. God has compassion on those who are too young to "know the difference between their right hand and their left" (Jonah 4:11).

- *Age of Accountability?*

We often hear of an age of accountability discussed in evangelical circles, but few seem to have any idea when this age arrives. Such uncertainty is not altogether unwarranted, though, because the Bible does not give us a specific age at which a child becomes morally accountable before God for his sin.

---

[30]If one's life is characterized by one or more of these sins, then he needs to take spiritual inventory and examine himself to see if he is truly in the faith per 2 Corinthians 13:5.

[31]See Isaiah 6:3 and Revelation 4:8.

This is not to say, however, that the concept is not taught in Scripture.[32] Some speculate that the age may be around twenty given that it was at this age when the young men in Israel were permitted to join their nation's army (Numbers 1:45). Others surmise that it is around age thirteen because it was then that Jewish boys were considered "sons of the Law." Though encouraged to follow them from early childhood, it was at the age of thirteen that they actually became accountable to the commandments. Some cite as support for this that Jesus was taken to Jerusalem by His parents for the Feast of the Passover at age twelve. It was here that He was "sitting in the midst of the teachers both listening to them and asking them questions" (Luke 2:46).

Though Jesus certainly demonstrated an unusual grasp of Scripture as a "pre-teen," if you will, I'm not sure we can extrapolate too much from that regarding an age of moral accountability. Jesus was, after all, not a typical child. He was God in human flesh and born of a virgin. His omniscience and lack of a sin nature did give Him just a bit of a leg up on the rest of us!

That having been said, I do believe the accountability of Jewish boys to the moral Law beginning at age thirteen is instructive. It seems that somewhere around this age is the time at which a child can become accountable before God for his sin. There is some biblical warrant for this being the age at which a child "knows enough to refuse evil and choose good" (Isaiah 7:15-16).[33] I would say, though, for reasons we shall shortly see, that this would be the earliest time this spiritual transition would take place.

Though I believe this to be a good rule of thumb, it would be unwise, in my estimation, to apply this uniformly to all children. Some children mature more quickly than others. We should be looking not for a hard and fast date on the calendar, but rather signs in the child that

---

[32]In a similar vein of thought, the term "Trinity" is not found in Scripture either and yet it is clearly biblical truth.

[33]Though this prophecy had its ultimate fulfillment in Christ (Matthew 1:23), it did have an immediate historical context in which it saw partial fulfillment in the birth of the prophet Isaiah's son, Maher-shalal-has-baz.

he has matured to the point he can understand the gravity of his sin and his accountability before a holy God.

Before this age is reached, however, little ones are simply not held accountable for their sinful nature or even sinful acts. Should they die, they go immediately to Heaven. Make no mistake, they are not saved because of any merit of their own. In fact, that is exactly the point. They are saved just as we are: solely by God's sovereign grace. They are saved by the sacrificial and atoning work of Christ on the cross. They must have the righteousness of Jesus Christ imputed[34] to them, just as we must. Their innocence does not save them. Grace does.

It is just that with babies and children, as a sovereign and gracious act, God imputes the righteousness of Christ to them before they are culpable for their sin and capable of grasping the Gospel. Let me further state that the mercy God extends to babies and children He also extends to adults who because of a mental handicap have the mind of a child.

So, if you are a parent of a little one who has died or of an adult child who through no fault of his own is simply incapable of understanding the Gospel, take comfort knowing that your son or daughter is "Safe in the Arms of God."[35]

---

[34]To impute means "to set down in a record or ledger." In and of itself imputation does not involve a change in moral character but instead denotes a change in legal status. The Bible speaks of three spheres in which imputation takes place: Adam's sin imputed to the entire human race, the sins of the elect imputed to Christ on the cross, and His righteousness imputed to the elect resulting in justification. The doctrine of imputed righteousness is a foundational doctrine of biblical Christianity and stands in stark contrast to the infused righteousness doctrine held by the Roman Catholic Church. In this erroneous view, the righteousness of Christ is infused through the communion elements (wine and wafer). These two views are irreconcilable and the difference between them is no less than the difference between Heaven and Hell.

[35]For further reading on this topic, see Dr. John MacArthur's book by this title.

The Nature of Children

Children and adults are not the same. They just aren't. You may be wondering why I would bother to make such a patently obvious observation. All of us recognize that there are massive differences between children and adults.

We do not expect children to seek gainful employment and hold down a job. We do not expect children to pay the rent or mortgage. We do not ask them to fix a transmission, build a house, or operate heavy equipment. We would not ask a child to prepare our taxes, nor would we trust one to give us medical care. We do not allow a child to drive, serve in the military, or vote. We are entertained watching a little girl have imaginary tea with her dolls or a little boy making engine noises as he plays with his Tonka trucks. This same behavior from an adult, however, would be a bit, well, odd to say the least.

It seems in practically every area of life, we have no trouble understanding that there is a sizeable gap between children and adults in their reasoning abilities, maturity levels, and responsibilities—except when it comes to the Gospel. In the vast majority of evangelical churches, as long as a child makes intellectual assent to basic Gospel truths and answers a few basic questions in the affirmative, he or she is deemed ready to be baptized.

Ephesians 4:14 says, "we are no longer to be children, tossed here and there by waves and carried about by every wind of doctrine, by the trickery of men."

Dear reader, nothing is in the Bible by mistake. The Apostle Paul, writing under the inspiration of God's Holy Spirit, compares people who are tossed here and there (or "to and fro" as the KJV renders it) by different winds of doctrine to *children*. By their nature children are easily "tossed to and fro." Scripture teaches this and simple observation confirms it.

Every parent will affirm how easily children can be tossed to and fro. What captures a child's imagination one week may be completely disinteresting to him the next week. A child will usually believe just about anything that is told him.

I can remember, as a child, desperately wanting a pair of cowboy boots. My paternal grandfather, "Pappaw" as my sister and I affectionately called him, had a farm in northwest Louisiana. Though not a cowboy as much as a small farmer, I imagined him as the former and I wanted to be a cowboy too. A good pair of cowboy boots would surely do the trick. But they couldn't be just any cowboy boots, they had to be *Justin* cowboy boots! (For you city slickers, "Justin" is a brand name for boots like Reebok is for tennis shoes.) I actually thought Justin cowboy boots were named after me. Egotistical, I know.

When I was two, my parents built a home on Great Lake Road in Vicksburg, Mississippi, where they live to this day. I can remember watching "The Today Show" in the mornings as my sister and I ate breakfast before catching the school bus. From time to time, I would hear Willard Scott, a long time weatherman for the program, talk about the weather in "the Great Lakes region." I can remember thinking how cool it was that Mr. Scott would actually talk about what the weather was going to be like on my home street! (I can also remember wondering why it never did snow all those times he predicted snow for "the Great Lakes region." My faith in Willard Scott as a weatherman began to wane.)

I remember asking my Dad what he did at work every day and he told me that he was an engineer. I could hardly wait to tell all of my friends at school that *my* Dad drove a *train*! The only problem was that my Dad was actually a civil engineer who worked at the Waterways Experiment Station in Vicksburg. Still a noble profession to be sure, but not quite as exciting as I had imagined.

Such is the mindset of a child. And all of these things I thought *after* I professed faith in Christ and was baptized at age seven.

The Bible gives clear testimony that there is a difference between children and adults. King Solomon tells us that "foolishness is bound up in the heart of a child" (Proverbs 22:15).[36] The Apostle Paul said, "When I was a child, I used to speak like a child, think like a child, reason like a child; when I became a man, I did away with childish things" (1 Corinthians 13:11).

In this text, the Holy Spirit of God carefully delineates the stark differences between children and adults. Children think very concretely. Adults have the capacity to think in abstract terms. Children take almost everything told them at face value whereas adults are able to make informed evaluations. Adults can utilize their knowledge accumulated over many years of life experience to make wise decisions whereas children just do not have that resource.

Granted, there is certainly no shortage of adults making poor decisions—all of us have made decisions as adults we later regretted. The point, though, is that children have neither the mental maturity nor the life experiences needed to make wise decisions on important matters. Whether or not they actually do, adults at least have the resources needed to make wise and informed decisions. Children do not.

Children also tend to think in the here and now, preferring instant gratification over delayed, but greater, rewards. There is an adorable video on YouTube demonstrating this tendency among children. Kids are put in a room seated at a table with an empty plate before them. A lady walks into the room and puts a single marshmallow on their plates and tells the child that he or she can either eat the marshmallow now or wait until she returns a few minutes later and then be given a second marshmallow to enjoy. If the child succumbs to temptation, no second marshmallow.

The hidden cameras are rolling, and it is entertaining, to say the least, to watch what these kids do when left alone. One child ate the marshmallow before the lady even left the room, but most did wait—at

---

[36] The verse goes on to say that the "rod of discipline will remove it far from him." The immediate context is the need for corporal discipline but the point is the same: It is the mental immaturity of children that makes such correction necessary.

least for a while. The children would look at the marshmallow, eyeing it from this angle and that. Some would pick it up and take tiny bites hoping their lack of patience would just not be noticed. One little boy decided to lick it so as to get a taste of the treat without leaving any incriminating evidence—smart kid! A few did have the discipline to wait and were rewarded with a second sugary snack, but most caved to the temptation.[37]

By their nature, children live in the here and now. They just do not yet have the capacity to make wise decisions that will impact their future. They have no experience in making difficult choices on weighty issues and cannot contemplate the potential ramifications on themselves and others for failing to do so wisely. If they have trouble resisting a marshmallow for ten minutes, how can they possibly be expected to resist temptation to sin or make a decision that will affect the rest of their lives?

Children are also naturally inquisitive. They have a natural curiosity about the world in general. They like to explore, investigate, try new things and ask questions—lots and lots of questions. Children raised in Christian homes will naturally ask questions about the things they hear and are taught at church. They will ask questions about why certain things are done. They will ask questions about God, Jesus and the Bible. This is good. This is how it should be.

But it would be premature to assume that this natural inquisitiveness is indicative of a genuine work of God in their hearts. In all likelihood it indicates nothing other than your child is of normal intelligence.

God has graciously granted me opportunities to preach all over the world. In fact, as of this writing, I have preached at least once on every continent except for Antarctica (No immediate plans to go there). I have been in countries that have sizeable, if not majority, populations of Muslims and Hindus. I have been struck by how many Muslim fa-

---

[36]Source: https://www.youtube.com/watch?v=Yo4WF3cSd9Q Accessed June 23, 2016. There are actually several of these type videos on YouTube.

thers dressed in their traditional Islamic garb I have seen with their sons standing right beside them dressed in exactly the same way. They are like little Islamic Mini-Me's. I have seen countless Hindu parents with the traditional red dots[38] on their foreheads with their children who also have the red dots on their foreheads.

These children have not made conscious decisions to embrace either Islam or Hinduism. They have simply adopted the religion and culture of their parents. A child's worldview is limited to the environment in which he is raised and it is to be expected that until he acquires the intellectual maturity to evaluate weighty matters and make independent decisions, he will simply adopt the belief system he sees modeled by his parents.

The questions that children ask are not reflective of a determined attempt on their part to evaluate their parent's belief system in order to see if it stands up to scrutiny or is found wanting. Rather, they reflect a natural curiosity and innate desire to please their parents and secure their approval.

The contrast between children and adults is not one to be missed. Matthew Henry in his commentary on 1 Corinthians 13:11 states:

> What narrow views, what confused and indistinct notions of things, have children, in comparison of grown men! And how naturally do men, when reason is ripened and matured, despise and relinquish their infant thoughts, put them away, reject them, esteem as nothing![39]

There is indeed a great gulf between the mindsets and maturity levels of children and adults. It is no arbitrary thing that the Apostle Paul employs this contrast in his letter to the Corinthian church. It is a contrast inspired by the Holy Spirit of God Himself, and, as such, warrants

---

[37]Known as a *bindi*, this red dot, also seen among some Buddhists and Jainists, represents the location of the sixth chakra, or, point of energy and a metaphysical concept of "concealed wisdom."

[38]Henry, M. (1994). *Matthew Henry's commentary on the whole Bible: complete and unabridged in one volume* (p. 2269). Peabody: Hendrickson.

our careful consideration of its theological and practical implications. It is there for our instruction and benefit.

Nature of Salvation

When one looks at the language of salvation in the New Testament it is rather adult sounding language, is it not?

The Bible employs three analogies in describing the Christian life. The first is that of being a soldier. Christians are to be ready to "fight the good fight" and wield "weapons of warfare" (1 Timothy 1:18 and 2 Corinthians 10:4 respectively). We do not send children off to fight wars. They not only lack the physical capacity, but they also lack the mental maturity for such an endeavor.

Secondly, being a Christian is compared to being a slave. Scripture teaches that those who are in union with Christ are "Christ's slave" and have been "bought with a price" and are commanded to "not become the slaves of men" (1 Corinthians 7:22-23). Entering into a relationship that means becoming the slave of Another (Christ) certainly implies an adult level of understanding and maturity.

Thirdly, the Bible describes believers as being "betrothed to Christ" (2 Corinthians 11:2). The Apostle Paul employs marital language in describing our relationship to the Savior. One's commitment to Christ in conversion is akin to one's commitment to his or her spouse in a marriage. Is this something a child can understand?

Most of us had puppy love when we were young. Suppose as a parent your eight year-old daughter came up to you after an afternoon of playing with her friends and said, "Mommy, I really like Tommy and Tommy and I are going to get married!"

Would you think this was cute? Sure! Would you think your little girl to be sincere in her feelings for Tommy and their plans to spend the rest of their lives together in marital bliss? Sure you would—as sincere as an eight year-old girl could possibly be about such matters. But would you then begin planning a wedding and call the church to reserve the sanctuary for the happy occasion? Probably not.

The New Testament uses adult sounding language when it comes to being in union with Christ. Consider the following statements from Jesus:

"If anyone wishes to come after Me, he must deny himself and take up his cross and follow Me" (Matthew 16:24). The term here for "deny," is ἀπαρνέομαι (*aparneomi*), and refers to no trite denial as, for example, simply denying oneself a chocolate chip cookie when the craving for one hits. Rather it denotes a strong denial, disowning and complete rejection.[40] It is the same word Jesus used to predict Peter's thrice-repeated denial of Him the night before His crucifixion.[41]

In other words, the way in which Peter rejected Christ, we must reject ourselves. Just as Peter publicly disowned Jesus, we must publicly disown ourselves. The Christian is called to "lay aside the old self…and put on the new self" (Ephesians 4:22-24) and "put to death the deeds of the body" (Romans 8:13). It is not that the Christian never sins, but that the true Christian goes to war against his sins so that he can live a life of obedience to the commands of Christ.

We must deny ourselves in our initial coming to Christ and continue to do so throughout our lives. It is a constant awareness of our total spiritual depravity and complete reliance upon the mercies of God. Arthur Pink states, "Growth in grace is a growth downward: it is the forming of a lower estimate of ourselves; it is a deepening realization of our nothingness; it is a heartfelt recognition that we are not worthy of the least of God's mercies."[42]

---

[40]Louw, J. P., & Nida, E. A. (1996). *Greek-English lexicon of the New Testament: based on semantic domains* (electronic ed. of the 2nd edition., Vol. 1, p. 452). New York: United Bible Societies.

[41]See Matthew 26:24.

[42]Pink, A. W. (2005). *Spiritual growth growth in grace, or Christian progress.* Bellingham, WA: Logos Bible Software.

How many children of grade school age do you know who deny themselves like this? For that matter, how many *adults* do you know who deny themselves like this? I would suspect none of the former and few of the latter.

The next phrase, "take up his cross," is even more sobering. Living in the 21st century, we have really lost sight of the impact of those words from our Savior. Today when we think of 'taking up the cross,' we most often think in terms of making it through some tough times. I have had a few people over the years come up to me and say, "Justin, you bear your cross well"—in reference to my handicap, cerebral palsy.

But my handicap is not a cross. Cancer is not a cross. Arthritis is not a cross. Losing one's job is not a cross. Having one's house burn down or even losing a loved one is not a cross. Are these tough times? Yes. Trials? To be sure! But is that what Jesus meant when He said, 'take up your cross'? Absolutely not.

When Jesus instructed men and women to 'take up their cross' two thousand years ago, people knew *exactly* what He meant. They had seen crosses in action. A cross was a place of death. A cross was an instrument of execution and an exceedingly brutal one at that. Jesus was saying you must be willing to die for the sake of the Gospel if called upon to do so.

Taking up the cross means that one is ready and willing to endure the shame of being a Christian. It means that one is ready and willing to endure the persecution that comes with being a Christian. It means that one is ready and willing to give up one's very life—both in a denial of self and, possibly, in a very literal sense.

We know both from Scripture and from records of church history that all of the Apostles, except for John, died for their faith in Christ.[43] They were martyred. History tells us of the brutal persecution and exe-

---

[43] Only the Apostle John was not directly executed for being a disciple of Christ. He was, however, exiled on the island of Patmos, the provenance of his writing the book of Revelation. He is the only apostle who died of old age.

cution of early Christians at the hands of evil Roman emperors such as Nero, Domitian, Diocletian and others. The Roman Catholic Church was responsible for the persecution and deaths of millions of Christians throughout centuries of persecution.[44]

Persecution of Christians is by no means a thing of the past. It continues today, unabated, in many predominantly Islamic countries. Christians are being forced to either pay a substantial tax for their faith, convert to Islam, or die.

In 2013, my friend and board member, Mike Miller, and I had a preaching tour in Uganda. Pastor Bill pastors a church in Uganda and he arranged a number of preaching venues for us across this poor, central African nation. Pastor Bill wanted me to present my seminar, *Clouds Without Water*, to help equip pastors in Uganda to combat the Word-Faith movement that is so rampant there.[45]

In the weeks leading up to our arrival, Pastor Bill was passing out leaflets in and around his village advertising our conference. A local Word-Faith preacher, one of the wealthiest men in the region, heard about the conference and monetarily bribed the police to put a stop to Pastor Bill.

The police found Pastor Bill, and right there in front of his wife and five children, beat him, arrested him, took him to the police station and chained him to a tree where they left him overnight—simply for let-

---

[44] The exact numbers of those persecuted and killed by the Roman Catholic Church varies widely, in part, because of the varying definitions of the Inquisition. There was a formal and informal Inquisition, spanning hundreds of years and covering much of the European continent and beyond. Taking a broad view of Roman Catholic persecution, the numbers are easily in the multiple millions.

[45] The Word-Faith movement is more commonly known as the Health and Wealth, or, Prosperity gospel which holds that it is always God's will for a Christian to be wealthy and physically healed. It is, tragically, the face of "Christianity" in much of the world today after decades of heavy promotion from networks such as TBN, Daystar, INSP, The Word Network, etc. My seminar, *Clouds Without Water*, is named after one of the ways in which Jude references false teachers in verse 12 of the New Testament book bearing his name.

ting people know about a conference at which the truth of God's Word would be taught. And this persecution came at the hands of a so-called Christian.

In Luke 14:26 Jesus said, "If anyone comes to Me and does not hate his own father and mother and wife and children and brothers and sisters, yes, and even his own life, he cannot be My disciple."

This is a startling statement. Was Jesus saying that we must literally hate members of our own family in order to be a Christian? No, not at all; for that would contradict numerous other instructions for us to love one another. The "hate" spoken of here refers to not pure hatred, but rather a lesser love. In other words, Jesus was saying that if we truly belong to Him, the love and devotion we have for Him should be so complete and unconditional that it would make the love and devotion we have for members even of our own family and ourselves look like hatred by comparison.

In May of 2016, Mike Miller and I preached in India, a country that is heavily Hindu. While there I spoke with a number of people who were saved out of Hinduism. One wife and mother of three small children said before she got married while still a teenager, her Hindu parents completely disowned her and kicked her out of the house once she became a Christian. They offered to take her back if she would renounce Christ and go back to worshipping their Hindu gods. She would not, and they did not.

Stories like this are not isolated. I have spoken to many, many believers all over the world who have been shunned by their families simply for being a Christian. I have spoken with people even here in the United States and Canada to whom this has happened. Sometimes people who get saved out of Roman Catholicism or the Word-Faith movement are ostracized by their family members who remain in these theological heresies.

The bottom line is this: being a Christian will cost you. Salvation in and of itself is free. It is a gift. It is given to us because we can do nothing to earn it (Ephesians 2:8-9). Once that gift is given, though, there is absolutely nothing in the Bible, nor in the history of the church that suggests that living a God-glorifying life will be easy or pain free. As I type these words and as you read them, untold numbers of our brothers and sisters in Christ around the world are suffering as a direct result of their fidelity to the Savior.

Being an obedient Christian necessitates that we deny ourselves, forsake all others, and even be willing to give our lives for the Gospel should circumstances call for it. We can't just pretend like Jesus did not say these things. He did. This is what a true Christian looks like. We are not exempt just because we live in a developed country in the 21st century.

I am a firm believer in the sovereignty of God in salvation. God has chosen a people to give to the Son as a love gift (John 17:24). He has set His affections upon them from before the foundations of the world and before time itself even began (2 Timothy 1:9). Salvation does not result from the exercise of man's will, but of God's (John 1:13). That God has chosen for Himself a people—the elect—is clearly taught throughout all of Scripture.

This having been said, the Bible also teaches the accountability of man. Jesus told the man in Mark 10:17-22 how to be saved and gave him an opportunity to come to Him, but he refused, choosing instead to hold to his earthly possessions. The Apostle Paul addressing the Areopagus[46] boldly preached that "God is now declaring to men that all people everywhere should repent" (Acts 17:30).

So, yes, God is sovereign in salvation and those whom God chooses for salvation will be saved. However, the Bible also stresses man's respon-

---

[46] Also known as Mars Hill, the Areopagus was a court in Athens, Greece at which Paul was asked to defend his teaching. The stone hill rises almost four hundred feet above the surrounding land.

[47] The tension between the doctrines of divine election and human accountability before God is what theologians refer to as an antinomy. An antinomy is when two seemingly contradictory teachings are both true. They seem mutually contradictory to us but only because our minds are finite and our logic fallen. In God's infinitude, they are not contradictory at all.

sibility and accountability before God.[47] We are to count the cost before 'putting our hand to the plow' (Luke 9:62). This is just not something of which young children are capable.

Summary

In this chapter we have discussed the question of what happens to babies and children when they die. We have also considered the nature of children and the demands of the Gospel. Allow me to bring these different elements together in ways that maybe you have not considered before.

If it is true that babies and children are safe in the arms of God in the event of their deaths, then why exactly are we baptizing them? Baptism is a public proclamation of an inward transformation; specifically, that the person being baptized has "passed from death to life" (John 5:24; 1 John 3:14) and has been "saved from the wrath of God" (Romans 5:9). So, if a baptized nine year old girl who dies would have gone to Heaven *anyway*, then what exactly is it from which she is being saved? If she would not have endured God's wrath for eternity had her life ended, then how is it that she was just saved…from His wrath? There is undeniably a significant logical fallacy in baptizing children.

We discussed how children by their nature are "easily tossed to and fro" (Ephesians 4:14) and that their reasoning abilities are far different than those of adults (1 Corinthians 13:11). We also discussed that the language of salvation in the New Testament is very adult sounding language: denial of self, taking up the cross, enduring persecution, and forsaking all others. These two truths make for a strong case against baptizing children.

Let me illustrate the difficulty. Many nine year old children still believe in Santa Clause. Many, if not most, children raised in evangelical homes are baptized by age nine. Are we really going to trust a child to make a decision about his eternal destiny when his intellectual capacity allows for the belief in a jolly fat man in a red suit who visits every home on earth in one night via a sled pulled by a team of flying reindeer? Can a child who believes in Santa or the Tooth Fairy or that babies come from storks really grapple with concepts such as the heinousness of his own sin, the futility of good works, the white-hot holiness of God, the fury of God's wrath, the meaning of the Atonement, the need for justification, denial of self, genuine repentance, counting the cost of following Christ and eternity?

I would submit to you that this is just not possible. Yes, children can have an interest in the things of God and the Bible. That is good and it is as how it should be for a child raised in a Christian home. This interest should be encouraged and nurtured. Nonetheless, this interest is not necessarily indicative of a real working of God's Holy Spirit.

Not yet. Wait on their baptism.

3

Heading our Homes

Under the inspiration of the Holy Spirit, King Solomon wrote, "Train up a child in the way he should go, even when he is old he will not depart from it" (Proverbs 22:6). Every Christian parent desires his child to know Jesus Christ as Savior and Lord. If this verse is true, why do so many children raised in evangelical homes mature into adults who show little or no evidence of regeneration having taken place?

Spiritual Leadership of Men

Guys, it's time we had a talk.

It is an undeniable fact that evangelical churches are baptizing legions of children who are not truly converted and new creations in Christ. That fact is what compels me to write this book. If all—or even a quarter for that matter—of the children we are leading into our baptisteries were truly regenerate, then our society would be far different than what it is. In the United States some 70% of people claim to be Christian.[48] If that were even close to being true, then we would not be slaughtering our unborn children in abortion mills and codifying "homosexual marriage"[49] into law.

---

[48] Source: http://www.pewforum.org/2015/05/12/americas-changing-religious-landscape/ Accessed June 25, 2016.

[49] I have this term in quotation marks because there is no such thing as homosexual marriage. God created marriage and He defines it, not the state. The United States Supreme Court may have codified something that it calls homosexual marriage into law, but it is not marriage. God has defined marriage as a union between one man and one woman for one lifetime. "Homosexual marriage," incidentally, does not bring the judgment of God, it *is* the judgment of God. Our society is experiencing the wrath of God's abandonment per Romans 1:24-32. God is giving people over to their depraved minds.

It might be tempting for us assign blame for the legions of baptized, yet unconverted, children on the churches. Our evangelical churches to be sure do bear a large part of the blame. Most have abandoned preaching the full counsel of God and instead deliver sermons that are little more than motivational speeches cloaked in a thin veneer of Christian lingo.

But, the churches are not the primary cause of this failure. The churches are the *secondary* cause. The primary cause lies at our feet, men.

Don't worry, I'm not about to fall into the "blame it all on the men" trap into which our culture has fallen. Our culture seems to delight in blaming men for just about everything these days. Men are either portrayed as knuckle-dragging intellectual oafs capable of being lead only by their base desires or true masculinity is mocked and men are emasculated into passive, effeminate, touchy-feely hippies.

That having been said, much (though not all) of the responsibility for the masses of baptized yet unconverted children amongst evangelicals does lie at our feet, men. At the beginning of this book I mentioned Charles Finney. Finney was singularly most responsible for introducing into evangelical thought decisional regeneration and what has become known as "easy believe-ism" or "cheap grace." Once his poisonous contributions to Christian theology and ecclesiology[50] took root some 150 years ago, men slowly but surely began to export their spiritual responsibilities to the Sunday School teacher or the youth group leader. This sad trend has continued largely unabated to this very day.

That men and women are of equal value before God is clearly taught in Scripture and is, therefore, an inviolable truth (Galatians 3:28). Men and women are saved by the same Gospel and have the same access to the same God through the same Savior. Men are not the spiritual superiors to women.[51] Men and women do, however, have different roles assigned to them by God.

---

[50] Derived from two Greek words meaning "assembly" and "word," ecclesiology refers to the study of the church.

[51] The very language employed by God in Genesis 2:24 that a man will join with his wife and the "two will be one flesh," language reiterated in Mark 10:8 and Ephesians 5:31, affirms the absolute equality of men and women.

God has ordained it that men are to be the spiritual leaders in both the church and in the home. In Ephesians 5:23 Paul instructs, "Wives, be subject to your own husbands, as to the Lord. For the husband is the head of the wife, as Christ also is the head of the church, He Himself being the Savior of the body."[52] The head of every Christian home is to be the husband.

Paul further writes in 1 Corinthians 11:3, "But I want you to understand that Christ is the head of every man, and the man is the head of the woman, and God is the head of Christ." No amount of hermeneutical gymnastics can get around the bedrock biblical truth that the husband is to be the head of the home. This is not in keeping with societal norms or mores. It is a source of scorn and derision for the politically correct class. But it is God's truth.

Note, though, the beautiful and majestic nature of this headship role. The male headship of the home is likened to the Headship within the Trinity. Just as God the Father is the Head of Christ, so also is the man the head of the home.

God is one God in three Persons.[53] Each of the three Persons of the Godhead is coeternal and coequal in character, nature and essence. In each Member of the Trinity is the absolute fullness of God. God the Father is fully God, God the Son is fully God and God the Holy Spirit is fully God. Jesus is no less God than the Father. Within the Trinity is perfect equality. Jesus said, "I and the Father are one," (John 10:30) and "If you have seen Me you have seen the Father" (John 14:9). In Christ "all the fullness of Deity dwells in bodily form" (Colossians 2:9).

---

[52]See for example 1 Corinthians 11:3; Ephesians 5:23; 1 Timothy 2:11-12, 3:1-5; Titus 1:5-6, 2:3-4.

[53]The doctrine of the Trinity is clearly taught in Scripture but is not easy to understand. Our fallen, finite minds cannot fully comprehend one God in three Persons but as Christians we do believe it because we are indwelt by the third Person of the Trinity, the Holy Spirit. He grants faith and illumines the meaning of Scripture to our hearts and minds. People in cults such as Mormonism and the Jehovah's Witnesses do not intellectually understand the Trinity because they, like us, have fallen intellects. However, they do not *believe* in the Trinity because, unlike Christians, they are not indwelt by the Holy Spirit.

Though there exists perfect equality within the Godhead, each of the three Persons does have different roles. God the Son does submit Himself in role to the Headship of the Father. Jesus said, "I do not seek My own will, but the will of Him Who sent Me" (John 5:30b). In John 14:28, He stated "the Father is greater than I." Jesus was not saying that the Father was greater in character, nature, or essence, but rather that as God the Son, Jesus willingly submitted Himself in role to the Headship of the Father.

This is the picture of marriage.[54] Men and women are perfectly equal in character, nature, and essence. One gender is not superior to the other. But, men and women do have different roles assigned to them by their Creator.

It is a tragedy of biblical proportions (pun intended) that the vast majority of professing Christian men today have precious little, if any, idea of what it means to be the spiritual leader in the home. Most assume that bringing their families to church on Sunday constitutes being the spiritual leader. If they say the blessing over the evening meals then that is *really* going the extra mile.

Kids in Sunday School? Check.

Say the blessing at supper? Check.

Teenagers attending youth group? Check.

Good to go, right? Wrong.

Men, being the spiritual leader in the home means that it is our responsibility to teach the word of God to our wives and to our children. In Deuteronomy 11:18-19, God instructs:

> *You shall therefore impress these words of mine on your heart and on your soul; and you shall bind them as a sign on your hand, and*

---

[54]For two excellent books on the biblical view of marriage, see *The Exemplary Husband* by Dr. Stuart Scott (Focus Publishing, 2002) and *The Excellent Wife* by Martha Peace (Focus Publishing, 1999).

they shall be as frontals on your forehead. You shall teach them to your sons,[55] *talking of them when you sit in your house and when you walk along the road and when you lie down and when you rise up.*

Men, are you doing this? Are you teaching your children the Word of God? Are you speaking of the things of the Lord "when you sit in your house and walk along the road and when you lie down and rise up" with them? Are you following the Holy Spirit's instruction to fathers in the household code of Ephesians 6 to "bring them (children) up in the discipline and instruction of the Lord" (vs. 4)?

Many are the fathers who train their children to be hard workers, to have character and integrity, who instruct them in the realms of politics and money management. Many are the fathers who instruct their children how to play sports, how to catch a fish or sight in a gun. Many are the fathers who will play dolls with their daughters and carefully examine any potential suitors as they mature into young ladies. Come to think of it, sighting in a gun and examining potential suitors kind of go hand in hand, don't they? *Just kidding!* Well, sort of.

But I digress.

All of the above endeavors are good and commendable! If you are doing such things with your children, good for you. Keep it up!

However, even if a father does all of these things with his children and then some, yet does not teach them the things of God and does not try to instill in them a desire to read and study the Scriptures for themselves, then he is failing at his most sacred responsibility.

Please do not misunderstand me, I am not against Sunday School —not at all. But the very best Sunday School teacher with the very best of intentions simply cannot do what God has designed the husband and father to do. The primary source of biblical instruction should not be coming from the Sunday School teacher, guys. It should be coming

---

[55] Though rendered as "sons," this refers to children in general, both sons and daughters.

from us. As the heads of our homes, we as men are uniquely tasked and equipped by God to teach His Word to our wives and children. This is not to exclude the responsibility of the wife and mother to teach Scripture to her children as well (Proverbs 1:8-9), but men must take the leadership role.

Not all families, of course, have the blessing of having a believing man as head of the home. If a mother is either a widow, abandoned by her husband, or married to an unbeliever then she must make the best of a less than ideal situation. She should teach her children the things of the Lord herself and trust God's promise that His Word does not return void (Isaiah 55:11). She will have the blessing of a clear conscience knowing that she has done everything in her power to teach her children the Scriptures. Do not underestimate the impact your obedience will have.

Paul wrote to Timothy, "continue in the things you have learned and become convinced of, knowing from whom you have learned them, and that from childhood you have known the sacred writings which are able to give you the wisdom that leads to salvation through faith which is in Christ Jesus" (2 Timothy 3:14-15). From whom did Timothy learn the "sacred writings?" Paul tells us two chapters earlier: "For I am mindful of the sincere faith within you, which first dwelt in your grandmother Lois and your mother Eunice, and I am sure that it is in you as well" (1:5). If you are a mother raising children without a husband, may these verses be an encouragement to you.

So men, do your biblical duty. Ready and study God's Word so that you can teach it to your wife and children. Obey it in your own personal life to adorn the Gospel and give it credibility. You cannot teach what you do not know and cannot model what you do not practice.

It should be noted, though, that it is possible that a father can be the spiritual leader in his home and still have one or more of his children walk away from the Lord as an adult. I know of some truly godly men who have taught and modeled Scripture to their children only to, sadly, see their children apostasize once they leave the home.

But at least these men have the blessing of having been obedient to their calling. They can take comfort in knowing that they did their best to fulfill Deuteronomy 11 and Ephesians 6. They should enjoy the inestimable blessing of having a clear conscience in this regard. Sometimes God graciously rewards us by allowing us to see some of the fruits of our labors. Sometimes He does not. Whether He does or does not, though, obedience in and of itself is always its own reward.[56]

Most professing Christian fathers, though, either through a lack of understanding, lack of equipping at their churches, cultural conditioning, or a combination of all of these factors, simply are not doing what God has called them to do.

Recall at the opening of this chapter I cited Proverbs 22:6, "Train up a child in the way he should go, even when he is old he will not depart from it." This verse has been a bit of a head scratcher for many parents. It is inspired Scripture and yet it is manifestly obvious that the outcome is not always congruous with what it seems to promise. The common interpretation of this verse has actually caused many parents untold grief and saddled them with tremendous guilt because despite their best efforts to 'train up their children in the way they should go,' their children still lived habitually sinful lives.

Might I suggest that the common interpretation of Proverbs 22:6 is actually wrong? Would it surprise you to learn that the meaning of this verse is actually almost completely opposite of the meaning most often ascribed to it? Bear with me.

The Hebrew word rendered as "child" by almost all of the English translations is נער(na'ar) and, though it could refer to a young boy, it generally refers to a marriageable male. It is more likely that it refers to an adolescent than a small child. If this rendering is correct, then the proverb is dealing with teenagers rather than toddlers!

---

[56] Read of the faith of those in Hebrews 11 who were obedient to God yet never saw the manifested reward of their obedience.

Another key point is that the phrase rendered as "he should go" is not even in the original Hebrew text and the word rendered as "Train up," חנך (chanak) is more accurately translated as "start out" or "begin." So, the more literal translation of this verse is "Begin a teenager in his own way, and when he is old he will not depart from it."

This more literal and accurate rendering puts the verse in an entirely different light. God is not commanding that parents let children choose for themselves how they would like to live. In fact, it is a warning against that very idea. Though many in our sin-stained world think that letting children choose their own way is "enlightened" and reflects the latest vogue trends of parenting, the Bible says otherwise.

Keep in mind that the entire contextual backdrop of the book of Proverbs is that of sin and its effects. Eric Davis, pastor of Cornerstone Church in Jackson Hole, Wyoming, states, "The book of Proverbs has the gravity of depravity running through nearly every verse. In the book the way of the fool is not unlikely, but inevitable, apart from diligent exertion in godly wisdom and discipline. To end up as the fool in Proverbs, one must simply do nothing; go the way of his nature."[57]

As stated in the previous chapter, every child is born with a sin nature. Left to that sinful nature with no guidance from a parent possessing the new nature via the new birth, a child will indeed "go his own way"—and that is not at all a good thing. A sinner going his own way always leads to ruin. And sin left unchecked and unrestrained is not only deleterious to the sinner, but to his family and society.

A child should not be left to go his own way. Allowing a child to go his own way is parental neglect. If a child is allowed to go his own way, then when he is older, he will indeed "not depart from it." In other words, he will continue in a downward spiraling lifestyle of sin. Proverbs 22:6 is not a promise, it is a warning.

---

[57]Article entitled, "Reconsidering Proverbs 22:6 & the 'Way He Should Go'" posted June 8, 2016 at http://thecripplegate.com/reconsidering-proverbs-226/ Accessed November 7, 2016.

So be the spiritual leaders in your homes, men. Teach your wives. Teach your children. Have designated times in which you sit down with them around the Word of God. Ideally this would be a daily routine. Strive for that. But, life happens. We are all busy and it may not be possible to do this every single day. If it's not possible, don't beat yourself up. But at the very least strive for two or three times a week when you can do this with your family.

Also, be sensitive to those everyday events that give you an opportunity to speak of the things of the Lord with your children. For example, maybe the news is on the television and politics is being discussed. You can say, "You know, kids, the Bible says that God raises up leaders and brings them down" (Daniel 2; Romans 13) and we are to pray for our leaders" (1 Timothy 2). Or maybe a friend or family member is sick. This is an opportunity to help your children understand that sometimes God allows sickness or afflictions to keep us dependent upon Him as David stated in Psalm 119:71.[58] You can teach them that life is full of trials but these trials often test our faith and can produce endurance per James 1:2-4.[59]

Even if a designated time of concentrated Bible study with your kids on a daily basis is not possible, opportunities to speak of the things of the Lord almost certainly will be. Make talking about theology and doctrine and the things of the Lord in general a natural part of your everyday life. This will help your children see that God's Word has saturated your own heart and it guides not only your conduct, but your thinking. Your children will see that God is not Someone to Whom we pay attention only on Sunday mornings.

And men, nurture your marriages. Your wife comes before your children. Your wife comes before your work. Love her as Christ loves the

---

[58]Psalm 119:71, "It is good for me that I was afflicted, that I may learn Your statutes."

[59]James 1:2-4, "Consider it all joy, my brethren, when you encounter various trials, knowing that the testing of your faith produces endurance. And let endurance have its perfect result, so that you may be perfect and complete, lacking in nothing."

church.[60] Love her, honor her, respect her, praise her. Let your children see you do these things. Lead by example.

And, men—be encouraged! You have the inerrant, infallible, sufficient Word of God at your disposal. You are indwelt by the third Person of the Triune God, His Holy Spirit, Who will illumine the meaning of the Scriptures to you heart and mind. He will empower you to obey them. He will equip you for your task to the glory of God. You are not alone, men!

Summary

It should be obvious to even the casual observer that most of the children being baptized in evangelical churches do not grow up to lead lives commensurate with their childhood professions of faith. Some may maintain a casual relationship with "Christianity" and church but their lives are not markedly different from their unsaved peers. One of the primary reasons for this is that few men are fulfilling their God-given role as the spiritual leader. Maybe you are a father reading this and realize you need to step up to the plate. Praise the Lord! It's not too late. There are resources out there that can help equip you to lead your home.[61] Even if your kids are already grown and out of the house, you can acknowledge your failure to them and ask for their forgiveness. Such a humble admission will give you credibility to be a meaningful spiritual example to them even in adulthood.

---

[60] See Ephesians 5:25-27.

[61] *Generations of Grace* is one such excellent curriculum designed for kids aged 3-12. See www.generationsofgrace.com

4

Looking for Fruit:
How to Know When Salvation Has Come

No Christian parent would knowingly baptize his child before regeneration has been wrought in his heart, but ascertaining when and if the miracle of the new birth has actually taken place in a child is an endeavor fraught with peril. The nature of children discussed in chapter two makes detection of regeneration very difficult. This chapter will examine some of the fruits that are in keeping with genuine repentance and saving faith.

Evidences of Conversion

One of the wondrous things about conversion is that it should look pretty much the same in all people regardless of their age. Whether we are talking about an eighty five year-old senior adult in the sunset of life or a sixteen year old teenager still in high school, conversion should look pretty much the same in both. A young person who gets saved does not receive a junior Holy Spirit. If a young person is converted, then he is indwelt by the same Holy Spirit who indwells an adult.

If a person has been made alive in Christ and has passed from death to life, there will be evidences of this supernatural transformation. The following is not necessarily a comprehensive list, and it should be kept in mind that each of the evidences of salvation is not isolated unto itself but rather is inextricably connected to the others. In other words, a person who is converted will display not just one or two of the following hallmarks of being regenerate, but each of them:

Change—When a person is converted there will be a marked change in his life. It is simply not possible for a person to be dead in his Adamic nature and then be made alive in Christ and there be no change. The Apostle Paul states, "Therefore if anyone is in Christ, he is a new creature; the old things passed away; behold, new things have come" (2 Corinthians 5:17). This change is no temporary effort of self-reformation. It is a supernatural change that can only be wrought by the working of the third Member of the triune Godhead, the Holy Spirit of God Himself. As such, it will be evident to others and it will be permanent.

What happens to many people is they have some experience in their lives which prompts them to make an emotional decision for Christ. There is a temporary change in thinking and behavior but it does not last because it is just that—emotional. It is nothing more than a Christianized version of a New Year's resolution. It does not last because it originates from fallen flesh. But that which is truly wrought of God's Holy Spirit will remain. "New things have come" in the Greek grammar suggests a present and abiding reality that will not fade with time.

The miracle of the new birth is just that—a miracle. It is a far greater miracle than the blind seeing or the lame walking. It is not something that we can gin up on our own. It is external to us. It is given, sustained and secured by God. A changed heart and life stand as testimony to this miraculous work of God.

Godly Sorrow—The Bible speaks of two kinds of sorrow over sin: a worldly sorrow and a godly sorrow. A worldly sorrow is horizontally oriented. In other words, it is centered on self. It is nothing more than a guilty conscience which everyone has.[62] A worldly sorry asks, "What would happen to *me* if my sin were exposed? What would be the con-

---

[62]The word "conscience" is derived from the two words, "con" and "science" which mean "with" and "knowledge" respectively. Everyone has a conscience and when someone sins he sins "with knowledge" that he is doing so. People need not to be told that, for example, lying, stealing and murder are wrong. Every person instinctively knows these acts are wrong which is why every person committing them tries to hide his tracks. A person's conscience can become seared over many years of unrepentant sin (1 Timothy 4:2) but all persons are born with one (Romans 2:15).

sequences for *me*?" A person with a worldly sorrow tries to hide his sin because he is worried about the possible personal ramifications that the exposure of his sin would bring.

Whether it is a young person cheating on a test, or a man hiding what he views on the television or computer, or a woman covering her lies, all of these actions are the actions of one with a worldly sorrow. This "sorrow of the world produces death" (2 Corinthians 7:10). Plainly speaking, the one who dies with only a worldly sorrow over his sin will spend eternity in Hell.

The other kind of sorrow over sin is a godly sorrow. A godly sorrow is vertically oriented. A godly sorrow is when we grieve over our sin because we understand that our sins grieve God—His Person. We desire to turn from our sins because we recognize that our sins grieve God (Ephesians 4:30) and we do not want to grieve the One Who died for us.

Recall that David, Israel's greatest king, committed great sin when he used his authority to sleep with Bathsheba and fathered a child with her. Then, to top it off, he had Bathsheba's husband, Uriah, sent to the front lines of battle. David secretly gave his soldiers orders to withdraw from Uriah at the heat of battle knowing that he would be killed (2 Samuel 11).

In this account, we see both a worldly sorrow and an eventual godly sorrow. Initially, David had only a worldly sorrow as evidenced by his orchestrated murder of Uriah. David thought that with Uriah dead, his sin would never be discovered. He did not care for Bathsheba, nor did he care for Uriah. And he certainly did not, at the time at least, care for God. His concern was solely about himself. He committed despicable sin and then lied in an effort to cover it up. Textbook worldly sorrow.

In contrast, the very next chapter records David's friend, Nathan, coming to him and confronting the king with his sin. God graciously used Nathan to bring David to a place of confession and repentance. One of the most beautiful examples of godly sorrow and genuine repentance is found in David's words recorded in Psalm 51:1-4:

1. *Be gracious to me, O God, according to Your lovingkindness; According to the greatness of Your compassion blot out my transgressions.*

2. *Wash me thoroughly from my iniquity And cleanse me from my sin.*

3. *For I know my transgressions, And my sin is ever before me.*

4. *Against You, You only, I have sinned And done what is evil in Your sight, So that You are justified when You speak And blameless when You judge.*

What an instructive passage for us. Upon first consideration, one might assume that no sins could possibly be more directly against man than murder and adultery. But that was not David's perspective. David humbled himself before his offended Maker. He knew that he had sinned against Bathsheba and Uriah, but he also understood that his sin was first and foremost against God. "Against You, You only I have sinned," said the humbled king before the King of Kings. David knew he had sinned against God and he grieved. A godly sorrow such as David's "produces a repentance without regret leading to salvation" (2 Corinthians 7:10).

Repentance—The Greek word for repentance, μετάνοια (*metanoia*), means to change one's mind. The predominant teaching among evangelicals is that we must simply change our minds about sin. We need only to admit that we are sinners and that constitutes repentance. Sometimes a basic instruction that we are to "turn from our sins" is included with the use of the word "repentance" which is good, but a bit minimalistic.

Genuine repentance is first and foremost a grace of God. In other words, repentance is in and of itself *granted* by Him (Acts 5:30-31;

---

[63]Initial repentance unto salvation must be granted by God but once in union with Christ, the believer is empowered by the Holy Spirit and can repent of sins as an ongoing part of his personal growth in Christ.

11:17; 2 Timothy 2:24-26). God must grant repentance because while still dead in trespasses and sins we are unable to repent on our own.[63] When a godly sorrow produces a God-granted genuine repentance, not only will our minds be changed, but our disposition to sin will be changed resulting in a completely changed life.

So, even though the definition of *metanoia* may mean a change in mind, that is not the whole story, or even the whole definition. It is the Holy Spirit Who placed words in the text of Scripture and the context in which these words are used is paramount to their proper understanding. It is the Holy Spirit Who determines meanings of words, not a lexicon or dictionary. Repentance is a change in mind wrought by God's Holy Spirit that results in a changed life before a watching world, and apart from repentance, there is no salvation (Luke 13:1-5).

Fruit—Genuine repentance produces genuine fruit. The Apostle Paul in Acts 26:19-20 said, "So, King Agrippa, I kept declaring that (all people) should repent and turn to God performing deeds appropriate to repentance." This does not mean that we perform deeds in order to repent, as that would be a works salvation, but rather that when God grants repentance, there will be deeds—fruit—in keeping with repentance. John the Baptist said, "Bear fruit, therefore, in keeping with repentance" (Matthew 3:8).

Jesus said in John 15:5, "I am the vine, you are the branches; he who abides in Me and I in him, he bears much fruit, for apart from Me you can do nothing." Every Christian will bear fruit. Anyone who professes to be a believer but does not have genuine fruit is not in union with the Lord. Note too, that believers are not to just bear raisins. Jesus said His own will bear "much fruit." The newly converted, naturally, will not bear as much fruit at first. They may indeed bear raisins for a while. But over time, their fruit will increase and it will remain.

Godly Affections—One of the evidences of genuine conversion is godly affections. He will love the things the Lord loves and hate the things the Lord hates. The Apostle John instructs his readers, "Do not love the world nor the things of the world. If anyone loves the world, the love of the Father is not in Him" (1 John 2:15).

In this passage, "world" does not refer to physical things like a good meal or a nice ATV ride through the mountains. Being a Christian does not mean we cannot enjoy and appreciate some of the simpler things of life. Rather, it refers to the invisible evil system presided over by Satan that is set in opposition to God.[64] The one who has been made a new creature in Christ will find himself loving what God loves because he has become a "partaker of the divine nature" (2 Peter 1:4). The new birth results in a deep and abiding affection for the things of God.

Personal Holiness—Every Christian's life should be marked by an increasing pattern of personal holiness. Before conversion a person has no innate ability to turn from sin in any meaningful way. The sinner is neither willing nor able to turn from his sin. He, like Lazarus four days dead in the tomb, must be called forth.[65]

The Christian, however, is not in this helpless state. He has been made willing and able to turn from sin by the regeneration and indwelling of the Holy Spirit. A Christian is no longer powerless against temptation. Temptation will certainly come, but God will not allow one of His children to be tempted "beyond what (you) are able, but with the temptation will provide the way of escape also, so that you will be able to endure it" (1 Corinthians 10:13).

There are those who teach that, once converted, a true Christian will never sin again. This is a doctrine known as "Sinless Perfection."[66] They are wrong. One who believes in this doctrine does not understand the depths of the sin nature nor does he understand progressive sanctification.[67] A Chris-

---

[64] See John 12:31; 2 Corinthians 4:4; 2 Peter 1:4.

[65] See John 11:1-44.

[66] This is an exceedingly dangerous doctrine because it minimizes the gravity and deceitfulness of sin. 1 John 1:10 says, "If we say that we have not sinned, we make Him a liar and His word is not in us." This is a statement addressed to believers.

[67] Sanctification is the process of being set apart for a special service to God. It is the life-long process in which the believer cooperates with the Holy Spirit's aid to become more conformed into the image of Jesus Christ (Romans 8:29).

tian can and does stumble into sin, but a Christian does not swim in it. A Christian does not look for opportunities to sin. He does not enjoy it. A Christian is one who recognizes that though the old sin nature still dwells in him (Roman 7:20), he is to go to war against that old man and to be "putting to death the deeds of the body" (Romans 8:13).

The Bible says that "all liars will have their place in the lake of fire" (Revelation 21:8) and warns, "Do not be deceived; neither fornicators, nor idolaters, nor effeminate, nor homosexuals, nor thieves, nor drunkards, nor revilers, nor swindlers, will inherit the kingdom of God. Such were some of you" (1 Corinthians 6:10, 11). Note well the past tense, "Such were some of you." A life marked by habitual, unrepentant sin is not the life of a Christian. If a person lives such a life he has no reason to suppose that he belongs to God. He should "examine (himself) to see if he is in the faith" (2 Corinthians 13:5).

A Christian is not perfect by any means, but, over time, his life will be marked by an increasing level of personal holiness. Progressive and steady sanctification is one of the bedrock hallmarks of each and every person who has experienced the new birth. Salvation is not perfection, but it is *direction*.

Steadfastness in Persecution—This fruit of regeneration is closely tied to the one previously discussed. The Bible say that "all of those who live godly in Christ Jesus will be persecuted" (2 Timothy 3:12).

Not some. Not most. *All.*

If you, like I, live in the United States or another Western country, it is not likely that we will face any hard persecution for being a believer. By that I mean that we are in little to no danger of being arrested, having our property taken away, beaten or executed—at least not anytime soon. But many of our brothers and sisters in other parts of the world do face such persecution. It is a very real part of their everyday life.

That having been said, this verse does not have the exception clause, "unless you live in the United States of America." There are no asterisks beside the word "all." A person who claims to be a Christian but does not truly live a godly life may well live his or her entire life without being persecuted in the least. Such a person, though, is not truly a Christian. The biblical reality is if you "live godly in Christ Jesus," or in other words, faithfully obey the commands of Christ, you will most assuredly face, at minimum, some soft persecution. You will either be ridiculed at work, denied a promotion, possibly fired, or ill-spoken of by friends or family members. Something along these lines will come your way and likely, far more than once.

The child of God will remain faithful to Christ through this persecution—whether it is soft or hard. Writing to the church in Corinth, the Apostle Paul said, "...when we are persecuted we endure" (1 Corinthians 4:12). A distinguishing mark of a disciple of Christ is that though the persecution will be unpleasant, he will by the strengthening of the Holy Spirit endure to the end and be given a "crown of life" (Revelation 2:10). A false convert will buckle in the face of real persecution.[68] The one bought by Christ will endure.

Hunger for the Word—Another distinguishing mark of a Christian is that he will have a hunger for the Word of God: "Therefore putting aside all malice and all deceit and hypocrisy and envy and all slander, like newborn babes, long for the milk of the word, so that by it you may grow in respect to salvation, if you have tasted the kindness of the Lord" (1 Peter 2:1-3).

Writing under the inspiration of God's Holy Spirit, the Apostle Peter said that those who have genuinely tasted the kindness of the Lord will desire His Word for it is only by reading and studying His Word that we can know Him. Once He regenerates us, the Holy Spirit will cultivate in us a desire to study the Bible. One who has been saved from the wrath of God and redeemed from his sins will love the One Who saved him. We naturally desire to spend time with those we love.

---

[68] In the parable of the sowers Jesus said the one who has rocky soil for his heart "when affliction or persecution arises because of the Word, immediately he falls away" (Matthew 13:21).

We want to get to know them better. The only way to spend time with Christ and come to know Him better is by reading and studying His Word.

It is a sad reality that most professing believers now separate knowledge of God and love for God as though they are two separate spheres. And for many, the terms doctrine and theology have almost become bad words. You may have heard someone express a sentiment such as, 'Well, I don't need doctrine and theology. I just love Jesus.' That is a foolish statement, for it is precisely doctrine and theology that deepens our knowledge of God. When our knowledge of God is deepened, our love for God is deepened. In his letter to the Philippians, Paul writes, "And this I pray, that your love may abound still more and more in real knowledge and all discernment" (1:9).

The Bible never separates knowledge of God and love for God; it always combines these things. The one who professes love for Christ but shows little desire to read, study, and obey His Word does not love Christ nearly as much as he professes to love Him. A person who is indwelt by the third Person of the Triune God will have a desire to read Scripture.

Increasing Discernment—Given that the Holy Spirit will cultivate in the believer a desire to read and study God's Word, one of the fruits that will, over time, be born in the latter's life is an increasing level of discernment. With an increasing knowledge of Scripture comes an increasing ability to discern between truth and error and right from wrong.

In Romans 1:24-32 there is a list of sins that marks the lives of those who have been "given over to a depraved mind." These sins include homosexuality (vss. 26-27), wickedness, greed, evil, envy, murder, hatred of God, deceit, invention of evil things (vss. 29-30) and lacking discernment.[69]

This is a sobering passage, is it not? Think about this. Included

---

[69] Though the NASB renders this word, ἀσύνετος (asunetos), as "without understanding," the NKJV's rendering of "undiscerning" captures its sense.

among the same list of sins from which all of us would (hopefully) recoil: that of being sexually immoral, inventing evil things, murder, and hatred of God, is the sin of lacking discernment? Sobering indeed. Consider that the text is not speaking of "backslidden" believers or those who have just gone through a bit of a spiritual dry spell. It is talking about lost people. These are people who have been "given over."

When the Holy Spirit takes up residence inside a person He gives him a desire to read and study God's Word and the ability to obey it. If the Holy Spirit of God is strong enough to save us, then He is also strong enough to deliver us out of deception. The Holy Spirit loves us too much and He loves Christ too much to leave us in serious theological error. The person who is indwelt by Him and is reading and studying Scripture will inevitably grow in his spiritual discernment. It's going to happen.[70]

Love for the Brethren—"We know that we have passed out of death into life, because we love the brethren. He who does not love abides in death" (1 John 3:14). One who has passed from being dead in Adam to alive in Christ will not only have a love for God but also for His children, the brethren. Conversion produces a desire to do good, "especially to those who are of the household of faith" (Galatians 6:10) and a desire to "bear one another's burdens" (vs. 2).

One of the joys of my international preaching is that regardless of the culture in which I find myself, there is an instant bond when I meet like-minded believers. I have a kindred spirit with them that is so real as to be nearly tangible. It transcends all cultural differences and even language barriers. I have an instant, godly love for my fellow brothers and sisters in the Lord and they for me. It is truly a precious thing to experience. We are called to love all people, but there exists a special, God-given love among the brethren one for another. Jesus said, "By this all men will know that you are My disciples, if you have love one for another" (John 13:35).

---

[70] Of course, a person who is newly saved with no background of Bible knowledge will not have a great deal of discernment right out of the gate. It is not uncommon for brand new believers to get led astray by false doctrines of varying types. However, over time, they will grow in their understanding of Scripture and discernment will be the inevitable fruit.

Obedience—In our society love is most often associated with feelings. We love someone if we have warm feelings of affection toward him or her. This is not, however, how the Bible defines love. Jesus said in John 14:21, "He who has My commandments and keeps them is the one who loves Me." Jesus neither defined nor measured love by feelings or emotions. Biblical love is defined and measured by obedience.

I hear some people proclaim how much they love Jesus. I hear other people express concerns that they do not love Jesus enough. It has been an interesting observation of mine that many in the former group seem to lead lives that are most bereft of godliness and many in the latter group are often the most humble, obedient servants of Christ I know.

The only objective measure that we have of our love for Christ is our obedience to His commands. The only accurate barometer of our spiritual health is the degree to which we obey God. If we love God, we will obey Him. No matter how enthusiastically a person professes his love for Jesus, if that person is not obedient to what Scripture teaches, then he does not love Him. Period. It really is that simple.

Some have pushed back against the notion that our obedience to God is the only accurate measure of our love for Him. They claim that such a teaching fosters obedience out of duty rather than true love. This, however, is a false dichotomy. Does a faithful husband provide for his wife because it is his duty or because he loves her? Both. Does a faithful father discipline his children because it is his duty or because he loves them? Both. It is not an "either or" situation. It is a "both and."

So it is with our relationship to God. We obey Him both because it is our duty *to* Him and as an expression of our love *for* Him. And the depth of our love for God is manifested when obedience to the commands of Christ comes at a personal cost. It is far easier to put some money in the offering plate on Sunday morning in obedience to the biblical principle of giving[71] than it is to deny ourselves and take up the cross (Matthew 16:24). It is far easier to tell a stranger whom

---

[71] For the New Testament instruction on giving see 2 Corinthians chapters 8 and 9.

we may never see again that he must repent than it is to plead with a close friend or family member to do the same.

It is not that feelings are illegitimate and have no place in the Christian life. In fact, I don't see how it is possible to not be deeply moved at the very core of our being when we contemplate Who Jesus Christ is and consider the magnitude of what He did for us on Calvary's tree. But, feelings and emotions fluctuate. When severe trials come we are not always full of warm fuzzy feelings. This is just not realistic and is why our long term pattern of obedience to Christ is the only reliable indication of our love for Him.

If asked the question, "What is the opposite of belief?" it might be tempting to reply, "Unbelief." This is not, though, how the Bible would reply. In John 3:36 Jesus said, "He who believes in the Son has eternal life; but he who does not obey the Son will not see life, but the wrath of God abides on him." Notice Jesus did not say that he who does not *believe* will not see life; He said he who does not *obey*. The opposite of belief is not unbelief. The opposite of belief is disobedience. Those who do not know God are not those who do not believe in Him. After all, the demons also believe and tremble (James 2:19). Those who do not know God are "those who do not obey the Gospel of our Lord Jesus" (2 Thessalonians 1:8).

None of us obeys perfectly, but one of the clearest indications that the new birth has come is a life marked by increasing obedience to the commands of our Lord. It should be our heart's desire to obey Him. The Apostle John states it beautifully, "For this is the love of God, that we keep His commandments; and His commandments are not burdensome" (1 John 1:3).

A Testimony

In November of 2016 I travelled to Franca, Brazil to preach at a conference hosted by Calvary Covenant Church. One of the church elders is a man named Danilo Terra. Danilo drove me around and took care of me while in Brazil. The two of us spent considerable time together and enjoyed wonderful fellowship. Danilo shared his testimony with me. I was so moved by it that I requested his permission to include it in this book; a request he graciously granted. Though you will probably be able to tell that English is not his first language, I trust that his testimony will be a blessing, encouragement, and possibly even an opportunity of reflection for you:

> I come from a Family that practices Spiritism, according to Allan Kardec's doctrine. Spiritism is a pseudo Christian cult (I didn't know when I was in it!) that mixes some doctrines and portions of the Holy Scripture with reincarnation concepts, karma, talking with dead people and healing through rituals that "releases" the power of disembodied spirits in the physical realm.
>
> I was taught to practice Spiritism since my childhood. While Christian children went to Sunday School and public services, I attended a Spirit Catechetical School and mediumistic meetings, full of teachings about Spiritism doctrine.
>
> When the Gospel was presented to me, I was sixteen years old. My life was relatively good at that time—or so I thought—except for all of the changes and pressures that a youngster has to face: profession choice, girls at high school, rebellion against parents, striving to be "cool" among the social and cultural environment, first experiences with all-night parties, alcoholic drinks and friends' offers to use some "lite" drugs. This was my world, a broad road leading to sin and eternal damnation, something about what I had no idea.
>
> At that season I was finishing my preparatory studies to go to university. I had the privilege of a sound education in my country and was dreaming of a military career as an infantry officer in the Brazilian Army.
>
> On a vacation trip, I noticed that something different had occurred with my best friend. I realized that he, little by little, was less interested in the "cool things" of our age. During the travel we did not go to parties with girls, as we often had before, but to my surprise, he was reading a book. Guess what? He had never read absolutely anything, even at school—in fact, he used to paste in the answers to tests from me!
>
> To my greatest amazement, he was reading the Bible and began to share with me things that he was learning from a youth leader named Paulo Junior. Those things put a great question in my head, but I left all that aside. I wished to live my life having

not to be preoccupied with religious affairs. I was satisfied with the Spiritism's worldview, however some in some aspects I felt something was missing.

When we came back from the vacation trip, my friend talked about me to the youth leader (Paulo Junior) and they planned to evangelize me. Paulo Junior began to preach the Gospel of Christ to me, but all that information about God's Law, sin, Jesus' sacrifice, atonement, repentance and salvation made no sense to me. I was pretty sure that all I needed to do in order to get right with God was to give my best and, in what I couldn't do on my own, another reincarnation would solve the problem.

They kept presenting more and more arguments to deconstruct the faith that I supported. I can remember conversations in which I asked many questions and Paulo Junior answered one by one and, as if that was not enough, he presented new problems that I couldn't deal with. Nevertheless, from the heights of my ignorance and vanity, I disregarded his reasoning and judged all that "believer's stuff".

When I was taken for the first time to an evangelical service, I was full of reservation, having the assurance that it would be an awful experience. To my surprise, during the offering period, the pastor explained the biblical standard and reason for the giving and told the church about the needs of the building maintenance, what caused me to agree and lower the guard. After, in the preaching, I was amazed with the clarity and simplicity of the text explanation and the application the pastor made to the life of the people—I was not accustomed with religious discourse so reasonable and applicable. At the end of the service, the guys asked what I thought about it. With my peculiar pride I answered—externally—that I disliked the service and was not in the mood to come back again. However, inside my heart I was impressed with all the Bible explanation that pastor gave that night.

After few weeks, Paulo Junior invited me to a particular meeting with him at the church. He desired to explain some more things about Christianity. What I didn't know was that he and my friend had spent the weeks before in supplicant prayer and fasting before God, urging Him for my conversion.

When the conversation began, there were no debates, like the other times. Somehow, the Holy Spirit gave Paulo Junior tremendous authority, persuasion and grace – all together – that my mind was being convicted by the Gospel. I remember so clearly, as if it was yesterday, that he applied the texts of Luke 12:20 (Thou foolish one, this night is thy soul required of thee) and Matthew 16:26 (For what shall a man be profited, if he shall gain the whole world, and forfeit his soul?), telling that none of the things I valued—intelligence, cleverness, ability, the possibility of a military career—could compensate the eternal loss of my soul.

He said that my life was lost and separated from God; that my family was in the same path of eternal destruction that was waiting for me and, only through repentance of sins and faith in Christ God could give me eternal life.

Those words produced such a conviction of sin, that I can remember the tears flowing from my eyes—me, so full of courage and answers!—while he told me about the forgiveness and salvation granted by Jesus to all those who believe.

I can say for sure—with the maturity that now I have in the Gospel—that I left that meeting definitely convicted of my sins and, what was better, assured of the forgiveness and reconciliation with God. When I arrived home that evening, a new creature entered the house of my parents. How precious and sweet was that night and the following morning!

At the evening of the next day I decided to get rid of every Spiritism book and saints' images I had in my bedroom. I gathered all that stuff and threw it to the garbage. What belonged to my parents I stored in a hidden place, because at that moment, all that I desired was to put away every and each thing that enslaved me for years in delusions and lies.

It was precisely that day the persecutions for the Gospel's sake began against me from my family. My parents—who were advised of my chats with the believers—after having seen my bedroom cleaned from the religious items I possessed, exploded in anger and fury. They accused me of changing the family's religion—it was happening since two days only!—of desiring to join with fanatical believers and told me they would not tolerate such things in their house. I argued with their ideas caring nothing of my own—however with very little biblical knowledge and even less wisdom. All I got was an order to get away from Paulo Junior and a promise to be taken to a psychiatrist.

Many were the resistances I had to fight in the first two years of my conversion. My parents didn't allow me to go to the church; when I was hiding from them, my father was looking for me halfway to the church; I had three Bibles torn in fury attacks of my mother; my father said to my younger brother that he'd lost a son and wished not to lose the other. Once I was locked inside my bedroom and prevented from leaving. Sometimes I was beaten at home by my father and mother. On one occasion I was sent to the city of my grandparents for a week, in order to have no contact with the brethren and the church... My relatives also persecuted me, disdaining my option for a "narrow-minded religion," saying that it was just a phase in my life that soon would pass and I would see the time I was losing.

During this time, I was growing daily in prayer, alone with the Lord in my bedroom. I got a computer program that had the Bible, so I could read it hidden from my parents. Despite all the opposition, the Lord made me devour the Scriptures in three months. When I was able, I was with Paulo Junior and the brethren; those moments of teaching, prayer and communion were my great joys.

I had already abandoned the idea of trying to pass the exams for the Brazilian Army, because it was a long way from my city, where I was being taught in the Gospel. I passed the exams for law school and began the five years of study that the course required. Early in the first year, the temptations in college began. Parties, invitations to go out with the guys, proposals for drink rounds, teachers—most of whom were renowned professors, prosecutors and judges—constantly mocked the Christian faith and, of course, there was the constant seductions of girls.

One evening, at the end of the class, about ten or eleven people on my course—including some "nice" girls—tired of my refusals to hang out with them, were forming a circle around me and began to ask if I really believed that it was possible to be holy. I answered yes, by faith and dependence on Christ. So they—and the girls—asked if I was a virgin. I answered, "yes." A laugh burst from their lips.

They asked me if I was not ashamed to be in college and still have not experienced sex. I answered—embarrassed and humiliated, but staunch—that I would save myself for the necessary time until I could enjoy sex in the bonds of marriage, with the wife God would prepare for me. After that answer, they were disappointed, mocked me more and were one by one retiring. I remember the looks of disdain from them—and from the girls.

Almost fifteen years after these events, I know of an Almighty and All-Loving Lord, who has revealed Himself—and still continues, through His Word and fellowship in prayer—my sufficient Friend, Protector and Provider. At no time, by His gentle grace, did I turn back or backslide from His holy ways.

I stood at His side to see Him convert my brother through my witness and preaching; I could see college friends being converted and today they are serving as pastors and deacons; I graduated in law and was a successful lawyer for five years, until I left my own office and was ordained to the pastoral ministry, in a biblical church, with sound doctrine, pastored by Paulo Junior. I traveled—and continue to travel—throughout much of my country and the world, in ministerial work. I had the privilege, after many years, of having preached to, evangelized, baptized and discipled my dear wife—Soraya—a consolation and delight of God. Our first child, Flávio, has just arrived this year and has filled our lives and families with joy.

Today, I continue in the pilgrimage the Lord gave me, not knowing for certain which ways my Savior will take me in this side of Heaven, confident that He is able to keep my deposit and crown, which I hope to receive soon with all those who love Him more than their own lives.

Summary

A person who has been baptized into the corporate body of Christ by the regenerating work of the Holy Spirit will demonstrate not one, two or even most of the above fruits, but all of them. Every. Single. One. There are no exceptions to this. None.

This may sound like an unrealistically high bar, but it seems so only because the Gospel has been so watered-down for so long. Just like the proverbial frog in the pot of water being slowly brought to the boiling point, the diminishing of the Gospel over many years has come to be blindly accepted by most professing believers. Modern evangelicalism with its market driven church-growth strategies and diluted preaching has produced churches full of people who would not even recognize the biblical definition of Christianity.

Danilo's testimony should not be the exception, but the rule. This is not to say that we all must have come from the same background and faced the exact same persecutions as he in order to be genuine believers. But, all of the fruits that God has borne in Danilo's life, He bears in every believer. This is what conversion looks like. This is how a Christian lives.

Our churches are full of people who "will not endure sound doctrine" but seek "to have their ears tickled" (2 Timothy 4:3). We have reduced being a Christian to intellectual assent to some basic Bible facts, walking the aisle, praying a prayer, and being baptized rather than looking for the real fruit of a transformed life, love for God and His Word and a willingness to take up one's cross.[72]

---

[72]For an excellent book on what being a Christian really looks like see *Hard to Believe* by Dr. John MacArthur (Nelson Books, 2003).

5

Guidance from the Biblical Record

Paul wrote to Timothy and told him that, "all Scripture is inspired by God and is profitable for teaching, for reproof, for correction, for training in righteousness; so that the man of God may be adequate, equipped for every good work" (2 Timothy 3:16). Though most evangelicals certainly don't seem to recognize it, the Bible is not only authoritative, but it is completely sufficient for us in every doctrinal and ecclesiastical matter. Though you will not find a verse that reads, "Thou shalt consider baptizing children once they reach age…," a proper understanding of both biblical theology and history is sufficient for us to come to a wise position; a position that calls for great caution.

Yeah, But What About These Verses?

At this point you may be thinking, 'What about Jesus permitting children to come to Him?' There are three recorded incidences in Jesus' ministry in which He dealt with children.

The first is Mark 9:42 in which Jesus said, "Whoever causes one of these little ones who believe in Me to stumble, it would be better for him if with a heavy millstone hung around his neck, he had been cast into the sea." The pertinent question is, "What is meant by 'little ones who believe'"? If the passage refers to small children, then logically it must mean that they are in need of salvation and would, theoretically, die and go to Hell if not converted at that age. I do not believe Jesus was referring to little children.

A few verses earlier (vs. 36-37) Jesus took a small child in his arms and said to His disciples, "Whoever receives one child like this in My name receives Me." The Greek word for "child" used here is παιδίον (pronounced *pai-di-on*) which denotes an infant or toddler; certainly not one in need of conversion or one that could possibly comprehend the Gospel. Though He was literally holding an infant or toddler in His arms,[73] Jesus was not referring to literal children, but rather to genuine believers. He was using the small child as an object lesson.

A true believer is one who humbles himself as a child, recognizing that he can contribute nothing to his salvation. Just as a child can contribute nothing to his physical well-being, we can contribute nothing to our spiritual well-being. We bring nothing to the table. We must come to the Savior in humility, recognizing our own helplessness. Jesus was warning of the extremely serious nature of causing one of these "little ones," a new believer, to stumble into sin. If we carry ourselves in such a way as to be a stumbling block to other believers, we would have been better off to have been cast into the sea with a millstone tied around our necks. It is a very, very serious thing to cause another believer to stumble.

The second incident is found in Matthew 18:1-5 in which Jesus taught His disciples about humility. The disciples were concerned about who was going to be the greatest in the kingdom of Heaven. Jesus, "called a child to Himself and set him before them, and said, 'Truly I say to you, unless you are converted and become like children, you will not enter the kingdom of Heaven'" (vs. 2-3).

The lesson here is even more obvious. Jesus is contrasting the attitude of the disciples with that of a child. The disciples were concerned with rank and status, whereas a child is not. The disciples erroneously believed their good works would earn them favor with God, but a child knows he can contribute nothing. The disciples were self-reliant, whereas a child is well aware of his dependency upon others.

---

[73]In addition to the Greek construction, this could not refer to an older child or teenager given that Jesus took the child "in His arms."

This is what is meant by having a childlike faith. In order to come into the kingdom a person must humble himself as a child. A person must come to the end of himself and recognize his total dependency upon God. He must be "poor in spirit" (Matthew 5:3) and come to the Savior with empty hands.

The third and final incident is recorded in Luke 18:15-17. Parents were bringing their babies up to Jesus in hopes that He would bless them. Like parents today, they were concerned for their children. They wanted them to grow up and be faithful servants of God so that they would one day enter into His kingdom. They wanted Jesus to bestow a blessing on them.

The disciples rebuked the parents, believing this would just trouble Jesus and be a nuisance to Him. Quite to the contrary, Jesus actually offered a gentle rebuke to His disciples and said, "Permit the children to come to Me, and do not hinder them, for the Kingdom of God belongs to such as these."

This is a tender passage and certainly is reflective of the compassion and love God has for children. The word rendered "children" is the same used in Mark 9:36-37 and refers to babies or toddlers. This is no sentimental love, though. Jesus was well aware that children are born with a sin nature and even used them as an illustration of selfishness and rebellion in Matthew 11:16-17.

Here, just as in the previous incident, Jesus is giving an illustration of childlike faith. Babies and young children have no understanding of their sin. They have no knowledge. They have no obedience to moral law. They have no commitment to truth. They have no accomplishments. They have absolutely nothing to contribute to their own well-being, whether physical or spiritual.

This lesson would stand in stark contrast to the Pharisees who believed they were morally superior to all others and would gain entrance into God's kingdom by their own merits. They were full of pride and self-righteousness. In fact, this was the subject of the parable Jesus had taught just before this incident.[74] He concluded the parable by saying "...for everyone who exalts himself will be humbled, but he who humbles himself will be exalted" (Luke 18:14). The babies and young children provided the perfect illustration for true humility before God.

"To such as these" is not a reference to young children being able to count the cost of discipleship, coming to a place of genuine repentance, and placing their faith in the finished work of Christ on the cross. It is a reference to those who share in a young child's spiritual status. Just as a young child recognizes his complete and total dependency upon his earthly father, we must recognize that we are completely broken and undone by our sin and dependent upon the mercy and forgiveness of our Heavenly Father. It is "to such as these" to whom belongs the kingdom of God.

Yeah, But What About These People?

Perhaps you have already been wondering, 'What about those people in the Bible whom God called at early ages?' Indeed, there are some individuals mentioned in Scripture whom God called for a special service to Himself when they were young. These individuals have been used by some to argue in favor of baptizing children. We will briefly examine the four most often put forward.

The first is Samuel. Samuel was the last judge of Israel and marked the nation's transition from the period of the judges to the monarchy. Barren Hannah desperately wanted a son and tearfully prayed that God would remember her in her affliction. She promised the Lord that if He gave her a son that she would "give him to the Lord all the days of his life" (1 Samuel 1:11). Samuel was God's answer to her prayer.

As a child Samuel grew "in stature and favor both with the Lord and with men."[75] Though the Bible records that Samuel was a "boy" when

---

[74]This being the parable of the Pharisee and the tax collector recorded in Luke 18:9-14. The Pharisee was prideful and arrogant whereas the tax collector humbled himself before God. The former remained in his sin but the latter went to his house justified.

[75]Compare 1 Samuel 2:26 with Luke 2:52.

God called him (1 Samuel 3:1) this does not mean that he was a child. The word rendered here as "boy," נַעַר (na'ar) is the same word used to describe David when he slew Goliath (1 Samuel 17:33). David clearly was not a child but a teenager and Samuel likely was as well.

The second individual is Mary, the earthly mother of Jesus. The Bible does not provide her specific age but we do know that it was common in that day and age for teenage girls to be betrothed in their teen years. Betrothal could come as early as age eleven or twelve though in such cases the actual marriage would not occur until a few years later.

Mary clearly had an impressive knowledge of Scripture given that her *Magnificat* [76] contained numerous Old Testament quotations and allusions. In fact, in addition to alluding to the Psalms and the prophets, she also alluded to two of Hannah's prayers in 1 Samuel.[77] She displayed not only intellectual knowledge but also mental and spiritual maturity. Though we cannot know for certain, Mary was likely between fourteen and sixteen years of age.

The third is Timothy. Some have argued that he is an example of one who was very young and baptized because of Paul's statement to him in 1 Timothy 4:12, "Let no one despise your youth... ." However, this is a superficial understanding of the text. Timothy was likely around 15 to 17 years of age when Paul led him to Christ in Lystra on his first missionary journey (1 Timothy 1:2; 1 Corinthians 4:17). When Paul chose Timothy to accompany him on his second missionary journey, Timothy would have been in his late teens or early twenties. The reference to Timothy's "youth" in 1 Timothy 4:12 came about 15 years later (1 Timothy is dated around A.D. 64) when he would have been in his thirties. So, Timothy was not as young as we often think him to have been. It is interesting that as a pastor in his thirties, Timothy was considered to have been youthful.

---

[76]This is the title given to Mary's song of praise during her visit to Elizabeth and is recorded in Luke 1:46-55.

[77]See 1:11 and 2:1-10.

The fourth and final individual is the youngest example of childhood conversion recorded in Scripture—by far. This individual was converted before he was even born! John the Baptist was "filled with the Holy Spirit while yet in his mother's womb" (Luke 1:15) and leaped for joy while still in his pre-natal home when Mary greeted his mother, Elizabeth (1:41). If there ever was a candidate for baptizing a child, it would have been John the Baptist!

Are these examples biblical support for baptizing children? Not at all. A quick lesson in hermeneutics will help us sort this out.

Every event recorded in the Bible was a real event in history and happened exactly as presented. Every event recorded in Scripture is not, however, to be considered normative today.

Exodus 14 records that when Moses with outstretched arms grasping his staff stood at the Red Sea, God parted the waters to provide safety for the Hebrews and destruction for the Egyptians. But if I were to stand on the bank of the Mississippi River near where I was reared and hold aloft my crutches, I probably shouldn't expect similar results. Elisha made an ax head float in 2 Kings 6:1-6 by throwing a piece of wood in the water. If I were to try that, however, a wet piece of wood would be the totality of my results. In Numbers 22:28-30 we see a donkey talking to his owner, Balaam. But I haven't seen any talking donkeys lately. If you are seeing talking donkeys, I might recommend Proverbs 23:29-33 and Ephesians 5:18 as your next memory verses.

So, yes, every event recorded in Scripture is a real event in history but not everything is to be considered a normal or even occasional element of our walk with Christ. Samuel was called by God to be a prophet, but there are no more prophets today.[78] Mary was called by God as a virgin to give birth to the Savior. That is certainly a one time event. John the Baptist, the voice crying in the wilderness to prepare the

---

[78] The service oriented spiritual gifts such as teaching, mercy, administration, exhortation, giving, etc. are still in operation in the church today. The Apostolic gifts such as tongues, the interpretation of tongues, etc. are not. For an excellent treatment of this issue see Dr. Sam Waldron's book, *To Be Continued?* (Calvary Press Publishing, 2005).

way for the Messiah, was also a unique case never to be repeated. Taking the few examples in Scripture of people whom God called for a special service at young ages as a normative grid for us believers today is poor hermeneutics.

The Historical Record

The book of Acts gives us great insight into how the early church grew and was organized. It is noteworthy that in the early days of the church thousands of people heard the Gospel, believed, and were baptized. But of the thousands of people saved and baptized, not once is there any record of a child being counted among them. Not one.

Consider that Acts was written by Luke, a physician by trade,[79] who seemed to delight in providing great detail to the events he witnessed and recorded. In chapter after chapter, Dr. Luke records for us the conversions of individuals and groups of individuals. He records their baptisms.[80] But noticeably absent from any of these records are children. They are nowhere to be found. In each instance, Luke uses the term for an adult man ἀνήρ (pronounced *ah-ner*) and an adult woman γυνη (pronounced *goo-nay*. The joke I make to my wife that women are "goonies" has yet to elicit much amusement on her part.). Further, nowhere in all of the New Testament are children ever referred to as disciples; this despite the fact that children are mentioned at least twenty-two times in its first five books (the four Gospels and Acts).

Given that the book of Acts does not hesitate in recording for us not only what the early church did right but also what it did wrong; this is insightful. It cannot be that children were not present when the Gospel was preached. Undoubtedly, they were. It cannot be that children were not considered important. Undoubtedly they were. There is something to be learned here. The early church did not baptize children. It just didn't. The baptism of children is something new, relatively speaking.

---

[79]Colossians 4:14 refers to Luke as "the beloved physician."
[80]See Acts 2:38; 8:34-38; 10:45-48; 16:31-34.

At this point some may raise an objection by pointing out the instances of household conversions recorded in Acts. Acts 10:24-48 records the evangelization, conversion and baptism of Cornelius and his household. Acts 16 records the conversion and baptism of Lydia and her household (vs. 15) as well as that of the Philippian jailor and his household (vs. 33). Crispus and his household believed and were baptized in Acts 18:8. Another example is that of Paul baptizing "the household of Stephanas" in 1 Corinthians 1:16.

To argue that these passages support the conversion and baptism of infants (as some have) or children is an argument from silence as none of these accounts explicitly mentions either. There is no direct evidence to suggest that children were even present, much less included among the baptized. In fact, in some of these instances the Bible provides some clues that children were not present.

For example, the household of Cornelius was comprised of his "relatives and close friends" (Acts 10:24) which sounds more like adults are in view. It is unlikely that children would be his "close friends." Lydia and her household were baptized in Philippi (Acts 16:12) yet her home was in Thyatira (vs. 14), a city on the other side of the Aegean Sea and roughly 240 miles away. It is highly unlikely that she would be carrying young children with her on such an arduous journey—if she even had any children. Stephanas' household was comprised of those who had "devoted themselves for ministry to the saints" (1 Corinthians 16:15); a role which would clearly be relegated to adults.

Couple this with the unambiguous biblical teaching that only those who have been transformed by the Gospel (as we have already seen, a reality the nature of which seems incongruous with the nature of children) and the biblical support for baptizing children is tissue thin—at best.

The vast majority of evangelical churches routinely baptize children at very young ages. Growing up in a Southern Baptist church in the deep South I witnessed dozens of very young children being baptized. It is not uncommon to see a child walk into the baptistery on a Sunday morning and have to stand on a stool because the water is deeper than he is tall. In fact, a 2014 Southern Baptist Convention task force commissioned to study the declining baptism rates in the denomination found that the only age group which saw an increase in the number of baptisms was "children under five years old."[81]

Think about that. *Five and under.* This means that many Southern Baptist churches (and evangelical churches in general) are baptizing children that are barely out of the toddler stage. This should not be. A few years ago a pastor friend of mine with whom I was speaking on this issue said, "We as Baptists don't believe in infant baptism, we just practice it." Well said.

Some astute observers may object to delaying baptism for anyone who professes Christ as Lord because there is no such delay in the New Testament. This is true. When a person publicly professed faith in Jesus Christ the New Testament pattern is that he or she was baptized, if not immediately, very soon thereafter. However, all of those baptized in the New Testament were adults and all came from decidedly non-Christian backgrounds; two factors which led great credibility to their professions of faith.

The fact of the matter is that there is a wide gulf between the pattern recorded in the New Testament of the early church and that of the modern evangelical church. The evangelistic tactics so common in today's churches and Vacation Bible Schools has no precedence in Scripture.

So, What Now?

Thus far we have spent most of our time discussing the many reasons to wait on baptizing a child who makes a profession of faith in Christ. I want to conclude by discussing what a parent should do in light of all that we have discussed and offer some guidelines on when baptism should be considered.

Resist the Pressure—There is a very real peer pressure factor involved in children being baptized. This is a pressure, incidentally, felt by

---

[81] Source: http://www.christianitytoday.com/gleanings/2014/may/five-reasons-why-southern-baptist-baptize-millennials-sbc.html Accessed 07-01-16.

both the children *and* the parents. In most evangelical churches it is very much the norm for children aged ten and under to be baptized. Baptism for children has become more of a rite of passage than a public sign of inward regeneration. If your child passes this age without having stirred the baptismal waters, you may begin to feel pressure from other parents in the congregation to have him do so. I am not suggesting this is an *intentional* pressure levied by other parents of children who have already been baptized. It is nothing nefarious, but it is very real. Your unbaptized child is like the proverbial gorilla in the living room. Nothing may be said about it directly, but everyone knows it is there. People begin to think to themselves, "Hmm, I wonder why Tommy hasn't been baptized yet?" There can be an unspoken and yet very real pressure for a parent to allow his child to be baptized before he is truly ready.

There will also likely be peer pressure from other children. When a child sees all of his friends making a profession of faith and going into the baptistery, there is tremendous pressure on him to follow suit. Children naturally do not want to be left out of things. This is true whether it entails activities on the playground at school or activities at church.

Couple this peer pressure on both parents and children with how far the salvation bar has been lowered, and you have the perfect setup for baptizing legions of children before they even have the ability to understand the Gospel, much less having been transformed by it. This pressure must be resisted.

Maybe you are a parent reading this whose child has already been baptized and you are beginning to realize you allowed his or her baptism prematurely. What do you do if you have already made this mistake?

First, don't beat yourself up. Reading this book may be the first time you have been challenged to think of these issues from a biblical perspective. If you are worried you may have already made this mistake—that's a good thing! Your concern shows that you care about the truth. The important thing is what you do with the truth you now understand.

Let me share a story with you that may be of encouragement. In the summer of 2012, I presented my seminar, *Clouds Without Water*, to a small church in rural Arkansas. Early in the service, a seven year-old boy was baptized. It was a typical baptismal service in that the boy's immediate family as well as some of his extended family members were present. They were asked to stand so they could be recognized by the rest of the congregation. The pastor then asked the boy a few questions to which he replied in the affirmative and was dutifully baptized.

Though I was teaching on the Word-Faith movement, as part of my introductory session entitled "The Duty of Discernment" I always mention Ephesians 4:14 that says we are not to be like "children tossed to and fro" and use that as an opportunity to caution against baptizing children. Right after this boy's baptism and with all of his family sitting before me, I took the pulpit. I could not change my sermon just because of what had transpired moments before and so I proceeded to discuss some of the things about which I have written in this book. Talk about awkward! I had no idea how this was going to be received by the pastor or the boy's family.

After the service, the mother of the boy came up to my wife, Kathy, to talk to her. She was in tears. She said to Kathy, "I did not know these things until now and I realize we just made a huge mistake. We should not have done this." She was immediately repentant.

This is one of the marks of a genuine believer. A genuine believer may be in serious theological error or even sin, but when shown the truth from Scripture, he will bend the knee to it. It may not be on the spot as was the case with this dear lady in Arkansas, but the knee will bend.

So, if you are reading this book and you have a child whom you have already permitted to be baptized at a young age, say to your child, "You know, I understand things much better now and I realize that I (or we) made a mistake in allowing you to be baptized when you were so young. When you get older and understand the Gospel better and if you are truly walking with the Lord, then you should get baptized again. It will mean much more to you later."

Talk about the Cost—We have already discussed that though salvation is free, discipleship is anything but. All of those who live godly lives will face tribulation and persecution. Do not shy away from discussing this reality with you children.

On Resurrection Sunday, a year ago as of this writing, my wife, Kathy, and I attended services at Grace Community Church in Sun Valley, California, pastored by Dr. John MacArthur. In his sermon, MacArthur preached from Revelation 14:12-13 which speaks of the perseverance of the saints and how those who are dead in the Lord are "blessed." Much of his sermon he spent talking about the high cost of being a Christian. He pointed out that many faithful servants of God in the Bible suffered horrific persecution. He referenced Hebrews 11 which records that some were stoned, imprisoned, killed with the sword or sawn in two.

He spoke of those who will hear the Gospel and be converted in the period known as the Great Tribulation. It will be a horrific time on earth such as has never been seen before or will be afterwards.[82] God's judgment will be unleashed and hundreds of millions will die. Despite such unspeakable horrors, genuine Christians will persevere to the end. God will preserve them. He will not protect them from tribulation and persecution, but He will protect their faith and will secure their salvation. It is in this sense that those who die in the Lord are blessed. We are not promised a calm passage through this life, but we are promised a safe landing. The reward for their faithfulness through such tribulation and persecution is an eternity with Christ.

We were there that morning with a couple we know and their eleven year old son who were members of a church in a different city. At the time, their son (whom I will call Scott) had made a profession of faith in Christ. Scott had an impressive knowledge of Scripture for a boy his

---

[82]See Matthew 24:21, "For then there will be a great tribulation such as has not been from the beginning of the world until now and never shall be." Though it is my eschatological position that the church will be raptured before the Great Tribulation begins, there will be many who are converted to Christ during this dreadful time.

age and had even spoken with their pastor about what it meant to be a Christian. Scott wanted to be baptized and his parents were working on getting it arranged.

Scott's parents were not pleased with the sermon that morning because of how graphic and disturbing parts of it were. Scott's mother told my wife, Kathy, that the sermon was just too scary for an eleven year old boy and the subject matter too heavy for him to process. Later that day I said to Kathy, "If that is the case, then they have no business baptizing him." She agreed.

As earlier stated, though those of us who live in Western, developed countries are not likely in any immediate danger of being arrested or tortured (or worse) for our faith in Christ, we will still face persecution. Hard persecution is a reality for untold numbers of believers around the world right now. We should not sugar-coat the Gospel when communicating it to children—especially those for whom we are considering baptism. To withhold from them the potential costs of being a Christian is nothing short of false advertising. If a child trusts a painless gospel, he has not trusted in the true Gospel. If he is too young to be told of the costs, how can he be expected to count them (Luke 14: 28)?

Salvation is not about praying a prayer and walking an aisle. It is a result of a sovereign act of God and yet also calls for one to count the cost of discipleship. Being a Christian will cost all sheep who hear and respond to the Shepherd's voice.[83] It may cost some more than others, but all will pay a cost. Salvation is free, but discipleship is not. Our churches are full of people who have trusted a painless gospel and in an experimental fashion, have put their hand to the plow, but upon the arrival of life's inevitable hardships, look back (Luke 9:62).

---

[83]In John 10:27, Jesus states, "My sheep hear My voice, and I know them, and they follow Me." Though most often used as a proof text for hearing God speak to you outside of Scripture (something which He does not do, but that is beyond the scope of this work), this verse is salvific in nature. In other words, salvation is not God turning a goat into a sheep, but rather the sheep hearing and responding to the Gospel call of the Shepherd.

Thankfully, Scott's parents later came to the understanding that he was not ready for baptism. They were right. By God's grace he one day will be, but not yet.

Look for Fruit—We discussed the fruit of genuine conversion in the previous chapter so we need not go over all of them again, but keep in mind that each of the fruits with which we dealt should be present in anyone who has been converted regardless of age.

One fruit I do want to bring to your attention in a more detailed way, though, is that of personal holiness. Recall that a Christian is not powerless against temptation as he is now indwelt by the Holy Spirit of God. One of the marks of a genuine believer is that he resists temptation and, therefore, his life is marked by an increasing level of personal holiness. If a young person is converted, he will exhibit an ability to resist temptation in a consistent way in which his unconverted peers will not. This is extraordinarily difficult to ascertain in a child or young teenager.

A seven or eight year-old boy is not going to be tempted by alcohol and premarital sex. His mind is not even thinking along those lines. Add ten years to that age, however, and it is an entirely different ballgame. Then he will. And this temptation will only increase after he leaves home and goes off to college. A level of independence from home will increase the temptation to indulge his flesh.

There is a remarkably insightful passage of Scripture that deals with this very issue and it is found in Daniel chapter 1. Daniel is one of the most significant prophetic books in all of the Bible but is also full of practical truths. Though rarely thought of in these terms, the opening eight verses of this prophetic book contain great wisdom for us as we consider how to evaluate the validity of a young person's conversion:

> **1** *In the third year of the reign of Jehoiakim king of Judah, Nebuchadnezzar king of Babylon came to Jerusalem and besieged it.* **2** *The Lord gave Jehoiakim king of Judah into his hand, along with some of the vessels of the house of God; and he brought them to the land of Shinar, to the house of his god, and he brought the vessels into the treasury of his god.* **3** *Then the king ordered Ashpenaz, the*

> *chief of his officials, to bring in some of the sons of Israel, including some of the royal family and of the nobles,* **4** *youths in whom was no defect, who were good-looking, showing intelligence in every branch of wisdom, endowed with understanding and discerning knowledge, and who had ability for serving in the king's court; and he ordered him to teach them the literature and language of the Chaldeans.* **5** *The king appointed for them a daily ration from the king's choice food and from the wine which he drank, and appointed that they should be educated three years, at the end of which they were to enter the king's personal service.* **6** *Now among them from the sons of Judah were Daniel, Hananiah, Mishael and Azariah.* **7** *Then the commander of the officials assigned* new *names to them; and to Daniel he assigned the name Belteshazzar, to Hananiah Shadrach, to Mishael Meshach and to Azariah Abed-nego.* **8** *But Daniel made up his mind that he would not defile himself with the king's choice food or with the wine which he drank; so he sought permission from the commander of the officials that he might not defile himself.*

Allow me to set the scene a bit. The book opens with the first of three raids of the Babylonians, led by King Nebuchadnezzar, into the southern kingdom of Judah in 605 B.C.[84] Notice in verse 2 that "The Lord gave Jehoikim, king of Judah, into" the hands of the pagan king Nebuchadnezzar. This was something that God not only allowed, but indeed orchestrated as part of His judgment against Judah.

As was common practice for the Babylonians when they conquered a people, Nebuchadnezzar's forces took some of the "sons of Israel," young men who were physically fit, handsome, intelligent, educated, discerning, socially poised and who possessed obvious leadership qualities. These young men, likely between ages fifteen and seventeen, were the crème of the crop from Israel and Judah. They were taken from their homes and families, brought hundreds of miles away and placed right in the middle of the pagan King Nebuchadnezzar's court.

---

[84] The northern kingdom, Israel, had already fallen in 722 B.C. to Assyria. Israel had no righteous kings and ignored multiple warnings from God through the prophets. The southern kingdom, Judah, had a few righteous kings and held on a bit longer but it, too, fell completely and the Temple was destroyed in 586 B.C.

Nebuchadnezzar wanted to use the talents of these young men for his own nefarious purposes.

They were to enter a period of brainwashing in which they would be taught a new system of education, a new language, and even be given new names.[85] The latter is especially significant because their original names all pointed to the God of the Bible and their corresponding new names pointed to pagan kings and pagan gods. This period of brainwashing was to last three years "at the end of which they were to enter the king's personal service" (vs. 5). Nebuchadnezzar figured that this would be sufficient time to make them forget about their background and upbringing and reorient their allegiance to him.

Notice that Daniel and his friends had pretty much gone along with everything. 'Want to teach us a new language? Sure. Want to give us a new system of education? Knock yourself out. Want to give us new names? Whatever floats your boat, Nebuchadnezzar.' But when it came to the kings "choice food and the wine which he drank," Daniel and his friends said "No." They had already "made up their minds" that they would not defile themselves.

This is a really surprising statement when you think about it. They had not voiced objections to anything up to this point, but when it came to the choice food and wine, Daniel and his friends drew a deep line in the sand and would not budge. They would not defile themselves.

Putting myself in their shoes, I might have been tempted to think, 'Well, I've been taken from my home, my family, my friends and am now in a strange country with a new name, being taught a strange language and indoctrinated with a new system of education[86]—at least

---

[85]Daniel means "God is my Judge," and his new name, Belteshazzar, means "protect the king's life." Hananiah means "Yahweh is gracious," but his new name, Shadrach, means "command of Aku," a pagan Babylonian god. Mishael means "Who is what God is?" and his new name, Meshach, means "Who is what Aku is?" This is a direct affront and intended insult to God. Finally, Azariah means, "Yahweh is my Help," and his new name, Abednego, means "servant of Nego," another pagan god.

[86]The Chaldeans were the elite class of wisemen in Babylon from which Kings heralded.

I'm going to get some good food out of this deal! Nebuchadnezzar's prime rib over there looks pretty good!'

The king's "choice food" would seem to have been the lone bright spot in an otherwise most unpalatable predicament.

Why did they refuse it? For two reasons: One, the food in Nebuchadnezzar's court was first offered to idols before being consumed by people. To eat food first offered to idols was tantamount to paying homage and giving worship to these false gods and Daniel and his friends were having none of that. To have partaken of the food would have been to defile themselves. Second, I believe that Daniel and his friends knew that they would soon be tested and they wanted all the credit for their upcoming victory to go to God and God alone and so they refused the rich food and ate only vegetables and drank only water. At the end of the ten-day test, Daniel and his friends prospered and were healthier than the other youths who did partake of the king's choice food.[87]

You may be wondering what in the world any of this has to do with children and conversion. Allow me to explain. Notice that Daniel, Hananiah, Mishael, and Azariah were not the entire group. They were just four of those "from the sons of Judah" (vs. 6). We do not know exactly how many of these young men there were. Some historians estimate the group was fifty to seventy five. Some estimates are much higher. For the sake of our purposes here let's stay with the low-end, conservative estimate of fifty.

Fifty young men are taken from their homes all from the same region. They and their families knew one another. They were close to the same age. All of them had essentially the same upbringing. They had

---

[87] Rick Warren has made Daniel 1 into a health regimen entitled "The Daniel Plan." He asserts that Daniel and his three friends knew the king's choice food "wouldn't be a healthy diet" and so asked "to be allowed to eat healthier, and at the end of ten days, they looked better and were more robust than those who ate the king's menu." Source: http://www.danielplan.com/start/about-us/daniels-story/ Accessed July 6, 2016. But this misses the entire point of the passage. Daniel and his friends did not prosper because of the food, they prospered *in spite* of the food.

exactly the same culture and exactly the same religious instruction. They all shared the same worldview. No two people have the exact same personality, of course, but as far as how they were reared, it was essentially cookie cutter. How many of the fifty did not defile themselves with the king's choice food and wine?

Four.

These fifty teenagers were hundreds of miles away from home in a hostile country. They knew if they resisted, they faced possible death. Conversely, if they cooperated the potential of upward mobility in the Babylonian kingdom was there. They could be promoted.

Think of the intensity of the temptation these fifty young men faced! All of them faced the pressure from the Babylonians, but Daniel and his three friends even faced pressure from their fellow Judean peers. The other young men succumbed to the temptation and were eating the "prime rib" and drinking the wine. No one would have looked down on Daniel and his friends for going along. Their parents would never know. They were hundreds of miles away and it's not like anyone had a smartphone to snap a quick pic of Daniel and his friends slicing into the succulent steak to post on social media. It would have been so, so easy to cave. No one back home would ever know.

But One would know. God would know.

Forty six of them caved. Four did not.

From the outside all fifty of these young men looked the same. They all professed to believe the same thing and all professed to worship the same God. But when the pressure was on, less than ten percent of them were willing to count the cost. All had head knowledge of God, but it was only Daniel, Hananiah, Mishael and Azariah who proved their love for God by their obedience.

I have spoken with parents of young children who have allowed them to be baptized and these parents have assured me that they placed no pressure on their children to do so. They have said that, if anything, they have tried to dissuade them. They have put no words in their mouths. I have spoken personally to many parents like this in my travels. I have no reason to doubt them whatsoever.

But they also tell me that their children were "tested" before being baptized. Sometimes the parents do the testing. Sometimes the pastor tests them. Most of the time it is both. But the "testing" involves asking the child to put into his own words that he is a sinner and to pray some version of the "Sinner's Prayer" unaided.

Now, I would readily admit that when it comes to testing children in regards to salvation, this is about all that can possibly be done. But that, dear reader, is *precisely the problem*.

Let's imagine we could somehow go back in time and gather these fifty young men and place them in a modern evangelical church. Let's imagine we spend a little time with them and tell them about Jesus being the Messiah the Scriptures foretold and explained to them the Gospel. Let's further imagine we could ask them the typical questions asked of almost everyone standing in the baptistery on a typical Sunday morning: "Do you believe Jesus is the Son of God? Do you believe He died on the cross and was raised from the dead? Have you asked Him to forgive you of your sins and do you confess Him as your personal Lord and Savior?"

Would they have all answered these questions in the affirmative? You better believe it! They all had good doctrine and theology. They all knew the right answers. If Bible drill were an Olympic sport, team Judah would have brought home the gold. If any of those young men were competing against a typical evangelical today, the former would have run circles around the latter.

Were they all sincere? In all likelihood, they were quite sincere. What was it that brought their differences to light? Temptation and persecution. There is nothing that reveals the genuineness of one's faith quite like these two factors. For Daniel, Hananiah, Mishael, and Azariah they were faced with both in a very acute manner. All of their friends melted in the face of temptation and persecution. Only these four stood strong and did not defile themselves. Their faith in and fidelity to Yahweh was tested and proven to be the real deal. In a modern day evangelical setting, it is only these four who should really be candidates for baptism.

Do Not Hinder Them—So, what is the proper response when your eight year-old daughter comes up to you after Sunday School or after a day of VBS and says, "Mommy and Daddy, I have asked Jesus into my heart and now I'm a Christian." What do you do?

Well, the last thing you want to do is throw cold water on her. Remember, she is very sincere in what she believes. She believes in Jesus and she believes the Gospel. If she expresses faith in Christ this is something in which you should encourage her. Say something like, "That's wonderful, sweetheart! I'm so thankful that you are growing in your understanding of who Jesus is and what He did for us. I pray for you every day that God will draw you to Him. I want us to continue to learn and grow together."

Encourage her in her desire to learn more about the Gospel. This is a natural and expected desire to see in a child being reared in a Christian home. Remember, though, that your child's interest in the Gospel is not likely an indication that God is bringing her to a point of genuine repentance and faith. It is simply an indication that your child is of normal intelligence and is naturally inquisitive.

Remember, there is a big difference between a childlike faith and a childish faith. A childlike faith is the kind of faith that recognizes that one is broken and undone before a thrice holy God and can do nothing to save himself. A childlike faith is one that recognizes his utter dependency upon God and one that is willing to serve Him regardless of the cost. A childish faith is the kind of faith that allows for belief in Santa Clause and that Willard Scott is telling the entire nation what the weather will be doing on your home street.

Even this childish faith, though, you want to encourage and nurture. God made children to be especially teachable and malleable for a reason. This is the season of their lives in which you will have the most influence over what they will believe as they mature. It is your sacred duty as a parent to teach them the Scriptures and encourage them to continue to grow in their knowledge of Jesus Christ and His Gospel. Daily pour into your child a biblical worldview. Teach her how to read and rightly interpret God's Word. Talk of the things of the Lord with her on a regular basis, "when you sit in your house, when you walk along the road, when you lie down and when you rise up" (Deuteronomy 11:19). Use the circumstances and events of life, both good and bad, and relate them to the attributes of God. Teach her theology.

However, wait on her baptism. Tell her, "Sweetheart, baptism is a very, very serious commitment, and when we look at the Scriptures, the only people who were baptized were adults. Your Mom and I love you very much, and we want what is best for you. We want to follow the Scriptures to the very best of our ability. We are going to wait on your baptism until you are older, just like those who were baptized in the Bible. And when you are older, your baptism will be much more meaningful to you than it would be right now."

You know what is interesting about this? Children are given but one command in Scripture and that is to obey their parents. This singular command to children is repeated twice (Ephesians 6:1 and Colossians 3:20). If your child is converted, she will submit to your parental authority over her "for this is well-pleasing to the Lord."[88] She will submit to you because you are the spiritual leader in the home that God has given to her for her benefit and protection. And this submission to you will not be a begrudging one. If she is truly converted, it will be a willing and joyful one. She will want to obey you, because she will want to obey God.

When Should We Baptize?

At this point you are likely wondering, "So, when *is* an appropriate age to baptize my child?" Well, I don't think we can be dogmatic on a

---

[88]Colossians 3:20, "Children, be obedient to your parents in all things, for this is well-pleasing to the Lord."

certain age because the Bible never gives one directly. We have seen, though, that there is no record of a child ever being baptized in the New Testament. All were adults. If I were a pastor, I would rarely consider baptizing anyone under age twenty.

"Twenty? Really?" you are likely at this point incredulously asking. "This sounds so out of step with what practically every church is doing nowadays!" I know. It does. But allow me to explain my reasoning for this.

By recommending age twenty for consideration for baptism, I am not at all saying that God does not save anyone below that age. I believe that He not only can but that He does save whomever He wishes whenever it pleases Him to do so.[89] The Shepherd undoubtedly calls some of His sheep to Himself before they reach this age.

However, given the nature of children and the nature of salvation, it is extremely difficult to tell whether the response is an emotional one or an effectual[90] one.

Sadly, I know of many children who made professions of faith in Christ only to walk away from Him in their teenage and adult years. Not only that, I know of many teenagers who made professions of faith in Christ and actually gave very credible personal testimonies before the entire church at their baptism only to completely walk away from the Savior they professed within just a few short years, and some of these

---

[89] The Apostle Paul states in Galatians 1:15-16, "But when God, Who had set me apart from my mother's womb and called me through His grace, was pleased to reveal His Son in me so that I might preach Him among the Gentiles, I did not immediately consult with flesh and blood... ." This is a fascinating glimpse into how God saves. Paul had been set apart for salvation from his mother's womb and even from eternity past (See also John 17:6,9) but his conversion came at the appointed time that it pleased God to reveal Christ in and to him on the Damascus road (Acts 9).

[90] The effectual call of God is when God draws His own to Himself and regenerates them. Jesus said in John 6:44, "No one can come to Me unless the Father Who sent Me draws him." The Apostle Peter says God "called us by His own glory and excellence" (2 Peter 1:3). The general call of the Gospel goes out to all (Matthew 22:14; John 3:16) but is made effectual when God calls His own to himself.

teenagers had fathers who were pastors. These are men whom I know and who truly were the spiritual leaders in their homes. They taught their kids God's Word regularly and faithfully lived it out before them. And yet, tragically, some of their kids still walked away from the faith they so convincingly professed when they were younger.

One practical thing that can be done not to eliminate but at least reduce the number of premature baptisms is to have the candidate give his public testimony before the church. This should be done for baptismal candidates of any age, I might add. The vast majority of people baptized in today's evangelical churches are – at most – simply asked to answer a few basic questions in the affirmative. They are asked to affirm that they believe Jesus is the Son of God, that He died and was raised from the dead, and that they have asked Him to be their personal Lord and Savior. These things are affirmed simply by the candidate dutifully replying "Yes."

Instead of such a minimalistic approach to baptism, the candidate should be asked to give his testimony before the entire church. If he cannot in his own words testify as to how Jesus brought him to a place of genuine repentance and faith and how the Gospel has changed his life, then he is not ready to be baptized. If public speaking makes him nervous, then he can write it out on a sheet of paper and read it. That is fine. But the one who cannot articulate and publicly testify to the transforming power of Jesus Christ is not ready to be baptized.

Such an approach to baptism not only lends credibility to the candidate's conversion, but it also benefits the local body. Hearing credible testimonies can be of great encouragement to believers. I know I have been immensely encouraged by listening to people testify of the gracious work of God in their lives. Detailed testimonies can also serve to convict those in attendance who may themselves be false converts. Upon hearing someone else's testimony, they may realize that their lives have not been changed, and God may use that to bring them to a place of genuine repentance.

As stated above, a person giving a personal testimony in his own words does not guarantee that conversion has taken place, but it does greatly reduce the numbers of those baptized prematurely.

Even if you think age twenty is too high, at bare minimum wait until your teenager has reached his upper teens and has some level of independence and has demonstrated that he does not succumb to temptation like his unsaved peers do. There should be a marked difference between how he lives and how they live. Also, look for a desire to read and study God's Word on his own without needing to be told to do so. Does it seem to be natural for him to discuss the things of God with you? Look for a desire on his part to pursue holiness. As his parent, ask yourself, "Would he resist temptation and pursue holiness on his own if I was not around?" If you have reason to doubt that he would, then you have reason to wait on his baptism.

If your teenager does show these fruits, and you do have confidence that these fruits are real and are coming from a heart that has been truly transformed, and if his repentance is evident to all around him both inside and outside of the church, and he can articulate a credible testimony, then baptism may be considered.

Conclusion

The theme of this book seems very out of step with the overwhelming stream of thought and practice in evangelical churches. It is. The threshold for baptism laid out in this book seems like a very high bar. It is. But so is salvation. Were we in the first century church the threshold for baptism presented in this book would not have raised a single eyebrow. That is seems so out of the norm for us today is a testimony to how far we have lowered the doctrinal bar.

If you are a parent, I urge you to give what you have just read in this book serious consideration. If your feelings and emotions run contrary to what you have just read, I ask that you put them aside and focus on the doctrine. If what has been presented in this book reflects sound doctrine and theology, then it should be heeded.

We should be very cautious when it comes to baptizing children. Only God Himself knows how many millions of people have been led to believe that they are Christians simply because they have said a prayer and been baptized and yet show no real fruit of regeneration. We do our children a disservice of incomprehensible proportions when we tell them they are saved simply because they have made intellectual assent to the basics of the Gospel. These children grow up to become adults who never examine themselves to see if they are in the faith (2 Corinthians 13:5) and never see a need to make their calling and election sure (2 Peter 1:10).

Not only do we do our children a disservice, but we are also doing the Gospel itself a disservice. When a person is baptized he is telling the world that he passed from death to life, is a new creation in Christ, and now belongs to Him. However, if that baptized person is not converted, then he will live like the rest of the world. There may be a brief time of personal reformation, but it will not last. That person will eventually live a life marked by sins that should only be found among the unregenerate. When there is little if any discernable difference between the lifestyle of a professing Christian and the lifestyle of the unregenerate, reproach is brought upon the name of Jesus and the Gospel is sullied.

Perhaps reading this book has brought you to a place of self-examination. Perhaps you have realized that you were one of those children who made a profession of faith and was baptized but did not truly understand the Gospel. Of the people who share with me their testimonies whether in person or through e-mail, I would estimate that easily 80% of them have a testimony that goes something like this:

> "I accepted Christ when I was a child (often in VBS) and got baptized. For a while, everything was fine, but once I became a teenager, I was tempted with alcohol and sex. I went to church but I lived pretty much the way all of my friends lived. I went to college, got married and started my career, but I never really lived out my faith. Then somewhere along the way, I began to be convicted of my sin. I started reading and studying the Bible and listening to some sound preaching. I began to see sin differently and my desire to study Scripture grew. Things that didn't bother me before began to bother me greatly. I used to never want to talk about the things of the Lord, but then I began to talk about Him all the time. Before, I would not really take a stand for Truth, but now I do. I began to grow in my walk with Christ."

With minor variations here and there, this is the basic testimony of most genuine Christians I know. Not all, but most. Most evangelical preachers today would call this a "rededication." The Bible calls it conversion.

There are legions of genuine believers in our pews that have this story. What many are calling rededication is actually regeneration.

These changes of which so many people testify in their lives are evidence of the new birth. Some of these individuals have sought and received believer's baptism. Many, though, have not. They are saved, but they have not been re-baptized, or better said, they have not been *biblically* baptized.

Maybe you are one of those. Maybe after reading this book you see much of your own life story here. Maybe you are realizing that though you know you are a Christian now, you really weren't when you were baptized as a child. If this is you, may I joyfully encourage you to talk with your pastor and share this with him? May I joyfully encourage you to seek biblical baptism? You should do this as an act of obedience to the command of Christ. If you are a believer who has not received biblical baptism, it will be a hindrance to your spiritual growth. Notice I did not say it can, but that it will.

Though there is nothing salvific or mystical about baptism, it is the command of Christ for the believer. If we do not obey His command, it will hinder our growth in Him just as will any act of willful disobedience. If we do obey Him, that act of obedience is its own reward.

Your obedience in this will also be a great blessing to others. Do not think you are alone. You are not. In all likelihood, many of the people with whom you go to church are also in need of believer's baptism. What a powerful testimony and great encouragement your obedience to Christ will be for them. It just might be the spark that God uses to spur others in the congregation to be baptized as well or, possibly, even to bring them to salvation.

As I close, it is my prayer that God will use this book to bring clarity to an issue that has long been clouded in church tradition. It is my prayer that God will use this book to encourage parents to bring their children up in the "discipline and instruction of the Lord" (Ephesians 6:4).

If your children are grown and have already left the home but are not walking with the Lord, and this book has made you realize that they are likely not saved, it is my prayer that God will use this book to encourage you to tell them the truth. The most loving thing you can do for them is to give them the Gospel and call them to repent. *Do Not Hinder Them* by letting them believe they are Christians just because they were baptized as children.

Give them the Gospel for it alone "is the power of God unto salvation" (Romans 1:16) and pray that it will "please [God] to reveal His Son" in them (Galatians 1:15-16). Even if they are far away spiritually, keep sharing and keep praying. You never know when their eyes will be opened to see the Light. When, by God's grace, the Light does transform their hearts, their subsequent baptism truly will be a meaningful event that will beautifully adorn the Gospel of Jesus Christ.

About the Author

As an itinerant preacher, Justin is committed to the expositional preaching of God's Word. Justin has a Master of Divinity with Biblical Languages (M.Div./B.L.) and Master of Theology (Th.M.) degree from Southwestern Baptist Theological Seminary. He has preached and taught at churches, Bible conferences, and seminaries across the United States and in over 20 countries. Though far from his only interest, Justin is probably most well known for his seminar entitled "Clouds Without Water: A Biblical Critique of the Word-Faith Movement." Justin and his wife, Kathy, make their home in Sandpoint, Idaho and are members of Kootenai Community Church. He may be contacted through his website:

www.justinpeters.org

Made in the USA
Columbia, SC
16 January 2018